LENT
for
EVERYONE

LUKE

YEAR C

D1440278

LENT
for
EVERYONE

LUKE

YEAR C

TOM
WRIGHT

First published in Great Britain in 2009

Society for Promoting Christian Knowledge
36 Causton Street
London SW1P 4ST

Scripture quotations are the author's own translation.

British Library Cataloguing-in-Publication Data
A catalogue record for this book is available from the British Library

ISBN 978–0–281–06220–1

1 3 5 7 9 10 8 6 4 2

Typeset by Graphicraft Limited, Hong Kong
Printed in Great Britain by Ashford Colour Press

To

the Christian Churches
in the North-East of England

CONTENTS

CONTENTS

CONTENTS

PREFACE

One of the most exciting things that has happened recently among churches from different traditions is a new willingness to read the Bible together.

We have often been puzzled and saddened at other things that, so it seems, we can't do together, or at any rate not yet. But no church has ever said that we shouldn't read the Bible together. Catholics and Protestants, liberals and evangelicals, charismatics and social activists, Christians of all denominations – there is nothing to stop us reading the Bible together, and everything to suggest that it would be an exciting idea.

This little book was born out of that excitement and out of a sense, among some of us in the North-East of England, that a great way to do this might be a Lent project based on the gospel readings for the current year. In Lent 2010 that happens to be Luke, so that's the gospel we're using.

Christians from all denominations in the North-East of England have planned various events for Lent and Eastertide focused on our shared reading of Luke. But at the heart of it all is the invitation to anyone and everyone to read Luke for themselves. This book is designed to help people to do that, whether in this region or elsewhere in the country or indeed in the world.

The text of Luke used here is the translation from my *Luke for Everyone* (SPCK, 2001); but there are too many passages to be able to ponder all of them in the eight weeks we are planning, so I've provided a selection for you to focus on. I've also provided short comments to help you get into each passage and, equally important, to help you pray from within it – for the world, the church and yourself. (In case you're wondering, these comments are shorter than those in *Luke for Everyone*, and have been freshly written for this book.)

I am extremely grateful to my many colleagues here in the North-East, across the denominations and the whole region, for their encouragement. I look forward to sharing Lent with them. I am particularly glad to be able to thank my colleague Mark Bryant, Bishop of Jarrow, for his enthusiasm for the project, his care in advising me with the writing, and indeed the many suggestions he made, which have substantially improved the book.

All proceeds from this book will go towards the work of God's kingdom here in the North-East of England.

Tom Wright
Bishop of Durham

ASH WEDNESDAY

Luke 1.1–56; focused on 1.46–55

[46]Mary said,
   'My soul declares that the Lord is great,
   [47]My spirit exults in my saviour, my God.
   [48]He saw his servant-girl in her humility;
   From now, I'll be blessed by all peoples to come.
   [49]The Powerful One, whose name is Holy,
   Has done great things for me, for me.
   [50]His mercy extends from father to son,
   From mother to daughter for those who fear him.
   [51]Powerful things he has done with his arm:
   He routed the arrogant through their own cunning.
   [52]Down from their thrones he hurled the rulers,
   Up from the earth he raised the humble.
   [53]The hungry he filled with the fat of the land,
   But the rich he sent off with nothing to eat.
   [54]He has rescued his servant, Israel his child,
   Because he remembered his mercy of old,
   [55]Just as he said to our long-ago ancestors –
   Abraham and his descendants for ever.'

Think of the last time you badly wanted something to happen and had to be patient. Maybe you were waiting for someone you loved to come home from a long trip. Maybe it was an all-important letter that took for ever to arrive. Remember what it felt like, day after day, to feel your patience getting stretched thin. Sometimes, perhaps, hope seemed to run out altogether.

Then, one day, it happened. Or rather, the first tell-tale signs arrived. The plane touched down. The letter with the crucial postmark landed on the mat. And the celebration began – began in your heart and soul, and perhaps in your voice as well. Even before the person appeared, even before you opened the letter, you started to dance inside with joy, relief, excitement. Everything was going to be all right now.

Now imagine that waiting going on for hundreds of years, through the memory and imagination of a small, embattled nation. Put yourself in their shoes. Things have gone from bad to worse. Powerful foreigners have trampled all over us. The world seems upside down, with the rich and arrogant always coming out on top. But we've been promised that one day a new world will be born in which everything will be turned the right way up at last and we will be rescued. And the one who has promised us all this is – the creator of the world! Surely he can't fail, even if he keeps us waiting?

Then, one day, it happens. Or rather, it doesn't happen yet, but the first tell-tale sign arrives. A young woman, saying her prayers and keeping the family hope alive, is shocked to get a message. 'It's happening! It's happening now! And it's happening *in and through you*. You are going,' says the angel, 'to have a son. (Yes, I know, there's no human father in sight.) He will be God's chosen one to put everything right at last.'

Mary knows full well that a virgin, which she still is, can't be pregnant. So the small stirrings of new life in her body are the sure sign that the world's creator is doing a new thing. The letter has arrived on the mat. It's time for the celebration to begin.

The whole of Luke's gospel is about the way in which the living God has planted, in Jesus, the seed of that long-awaited hope in the world. It begins with that tiny life in Mary's womb. It continues with Jesus as a young adult planting seeds of hope around Galilee and Jerusalem. It climaxes with Jesus himself being placed in the dark tomb and rising again to launch God's worldwide project of putting the world the right way up. That's the story we are now invited to live inside and make our own.

Today

As you read Luke with many other Christians this Lent, come with your hopes and longings, your awareness of the ways in which the world is still out of joint. You might begin, today, by thinking about some situations, whether in your own life or far away, where the world is not yet right. Hold them before God in prayer and patience. And then look for the signs of hope around you, the first stirrings of God's new life. And give thanks to God for the way in which he is at work in the world today.

There's a long way to go. But the party begins here.

THURSDAY AFTER ASH WEDNESDAY
Luke 1.57–80; focused on 1.67–79

[67]John's father Zechariah was filled with the Holy Spirit, and spoke this prophecy:

> [68]'Blessed be the Lord, Israel's God!
> He's come to his people and bought them their freedom.
> [69]He's raised up a horn of salvation for us
> In David's house, the house of his servant,
> [70]Just as he promised, through the mouths of his prophets,
> The holy ones, speaking from ages of old:
> [71]Salvation from our enemies, rescue from hatred,
> [72]Mercy to our ancestors, keeping his holy covenant.
> [73]He swore an oath to Abraham our father,
> [74]To give us deliverance from fear and from foes,
> So we might worship him, [75]holy and righteous
> Before his face to the end of our days.
> [76]You, child, will be called the prophet of the Highest One,
> Go ahead of the Lord, preparing his way,
> [77]Letting his people know of salvation,
> Through the forgiveness of all their sins.
> [78]The heart of our God is full of mercy,
> That's why his daylight has dawned from on high,
> [79]Bringing light to the dark, as we sat in death's shadow,
> Guiding our feet in the path of peace.'

Pause, shut your eyes for a moment, and imagine. You are Elisabeth, the childless woman in the village. Everybody thought you were too old to have children, but now you've just had a son. You don't know for sure, but often you used to feel that people were pointing at you or talking about you behind your back. 'What a shame,' they seemed to be saying. 'It's so sad. Nobody to care for her in her old age.' Sometimes you wondered if they were saying that God had put a curse on you…

But now there's already quite a little crowd around you. Friends and neighbours have squashed into the little house, all excited and eager to have a peek at the little baby. Who's he like? How come it happened so late in life? What'll he be when he grows up?

But something else is going on as well. Your husband has been struck dumb ever since the news that the baby's on the way. Nobody knows what's going on but it adds to the strangeness, and the excitement. And then the moment arrives. *What's the baby's name?* Everybody assumes he'll have his father's name. But no: the father is doing something. He's writing something down: 'His name is John.'

No time to wonder why, because suddenly the old man can speak again. And, like champagne bubbling out of a hastily opened bottle, what comes out is a stream of praise. You find yourself caught up in it. All the old promises have come true, and this little baby is going to walk in front of them to tell people to get ready! God promised David a son, and Abraham a great family, through which he would rescue his people and the whole world – and it's happening at last! And this newly named boy, John, will be in the middle of it.

As you stand there, awestruck, can you sense something happening in yourself as well? Can you hear a voice, saying to you, 'Yes, it's true; I am doing a new thing; and you have a part in it!'?

Today

Sit there for a while, watching and listening. Join in the great stream of praise, but turn it into prayer as well.

Lord, where do I fit into this new picture? What task have you prepared for me? Where can I bring hope to the fearful, and daylight into darkness?

FRIDAY AFTER ASH WEDNESDAY

Luke 2.1–21; focused on 2.8–15

[8]There were shepherds in that region, out in the open, keeping a night watch around their flock. [9]An angel of the Lord stood in front of them. The glory of the Lord shone around them, and they were terrified.

[10]'Don't be afraid,' the angel said to them. 'Look: I've got good news for you, news which will make everybody very happy. [11]Today a saviour has been born for you – the Messiah, the Lord! – in David's town. [12]This will be the sign for you: you'll find the baby wrapped up, and lying in a feeding-trough.'

[13]Suddenly, with the angel, there was a crowd of the heavenly armies. They were praising God, saying,

[14]'Glory to God in the highest,
and peace upon earth among those in his favour.'

[15]So when the angels had gone away again into heaven, the shepherds said to each other,

'Well then; let's go to Bethlehem and see what it's all about, all this that the Lord has told us.'

As a shepherd, you'd be used to having the sheep follow you with a kind of blind obedience. In the Middle East, to this day, shepherds don't need sheepdogs to tell the sheep what to do. They just set off ahead of the sheep. The sheep trust them to take them to places where, in an often dusty and stony landscape, there will be water to drink and grass to nibble. So off they go.

Now imagine you were one of those shepherds out on the hills near Bethlehem, suddenly finding that instead of leading your sheep to where they can get food, someone else is telling *you* to go and find something – some*one* – who's lying in a feeding-trough! How absurd is that? Your first reaction might well be, 'This is some kind of a joke. I must have been dreaming.'

But no: all your companions have seen and heard it as well. So we have to be sheep, now, do we? Why is that?

Back comes the answer, sung to music the like of which you'd never imagined before: 'The great Shepherd himself has been born! The King is here, and you are his sheep, his people! Come and find him!'

And, as a sign that you're not just having a kind of collective hallucination, something remarkable and unlikely: the baby, when you find him, will be lying in a feeding-trough. You'll see, and you'll know.

Pause, and think prayerfully about what sort of decision it takes to do what the angels were insisting. This is quite crazy. Things like this don't happen – especially not to me. And, even supposing that this really might be the boy-king who would be the shepherd of God's people, it could be dangerous. Perhaps we shouldn't get mixed up in stuff like that. Better to lie low, to stay quiet, keep your head down.

But then…supposing this was the moment towards which your whole life had been leading? And supposing you messed it up and missed it out? You wouldn't want to spend the rest of your days kicking yourself for not being there at the most important moment in your own life.

So off you go. And it's true, however unlikely. There is the baby, in the feeding-trough. The message was right. So they really *were* angels after all. And – equally unlikely – so this really *is* the boy-king, David's son. To think you might have shrugged your shoulders and not turned up!

Today

Pause and pray about the quiet messages you get from time to time; perhaps not angels singing, but a soft whisper that tells you to go somewhere unexpected, to do something you hadn't planned, to visit someone you weren't previously thinking about.

Lord, let me be ready to hear your voice. And let me be eager to obey, to come and worship.

SATURDAY AFTER ASH WEDNESDAY

Luke 4.1–13

¹Jesus returned from the Jordan, filled with the Spirit. The Spirit took him off into the wilderness ²for forty days, to be tested by the devil. He ate nothing during that time, and at the end of it he was hungry.

³'If you are God's son,' said the devil, 'tell this stone to become a loaf of bread.'

⁴'It is written,' replied Jesus, '"It takes more than bread to keep you alive."'

⁵The devil then took him up and showed him, in an instant, all the kingdoms of the world.

⁶'I will give you authority over all of this,' said the devil, 'and all the prestige that goes with it. It's been given to me, you see, and I give it to anyone I like. ⁷So it can all be yours... if you will just worship me.'

⁸'It is written,' replied Jesus, '"The Lord your God is the one you must worship; he is the only one you must serve."'

⁹Then the devil took him to Jerusalem, and stood him on a pinnacle of the Temple.

'If you are God's son,' he said, 'throw yourself down from here; [10]it's written that "He will give his angels a command about you, to look after you"; [11]and "They will carry you in their hands, so that you won't hit your foot against a stone."'

[12]'It has been said,' replied Jesus, '"You mustn't put your God to the test."'

[13]When the devil had finished each temptation, he left him until another opportunity.

I saw an advertisement the other day for a particular car. The makers were very proud of the fact that this car had been put through all kinds of tests to see what would happen to it under the most extreme conditions. The car had come through with flying colours.

That's what you do with a car. But we don't often think about it happening to you and me. And yet that's what this passage is about. It's about Jesus going through the test, and coming through with flying colours. And since it's a test we have all failed, it's worth pondering, prayerfully, what Jesus was actually achieving and how it can help us, this Lent and throughout our lives.

What was it like, being Jesus? That's a huge and difficult question, but Luke wants us at least to try imagining the scene as though it was happening to ourselves.

First, he was very hungry; but he had learned self-control over his own body.

Second, he knew (because he'd just been told at his baptism) that he was indeed the one whom God was calling to be Messiah, King of Israel and the world; but there was a right way and a wrong way of becoming what God wanted him to be.

Third, he knew he had to bring God's people on side with what he was called to do; but again there would be a right and a wrong way of doing that.

To say 'this can't have been easy' is a huge understatement. There is a sense in this story of a deep wrestling, a heart-searching, a personal struggle with the powerful pull of bodily appetites, ambition and prestige. Most of us know only a little of that struggle, because we tend to give up and give in, early on in the process. Jesus went all the way through the tests and still didn't break.

That is part of the point for us now. This is the start of Jesus' own story, pointing already to the cross where he will hang in humiliation, powerless, his body tortured to destruction. But Luke encourages us to hear its echoes in our own story.

Today

Stand there beside Jesus as he faces those tests.

What tests are you facing right now? How are the whispering voices trying to lure you off course, into doing the right thing in the wrong way, or the wrong thing altogether? Where will you look in scripture to find help and strength?

Lord, give me the strength not to give up; to reach for your word, to remember what you are calling me to be and to do and, with your help, to persevere through whatever tests may come.

WEEK 1: SUNDAY

Psalm 91.1–2, 9–16

¹You who live in the shelter of the Most High,
  Who abide in the shadow of the Almighty,
²will say to the Lord, 'My refuge and my fortress;
  my God, in whom I trust.'…
⁹Because you have made the Lord your refuge,
  the Most High your dwelling-place,
¹⁰no evil shall befall you,
  no scourge come near your tent.
¹¹For he will command his angels concerning you
  to guard you in all your ways.
¹²On their hands they will bear you up,
  so that you will not dash your foot against a stone.

¹³You will tread on the lion and the adder,
  the young lion and the serpent you will trample under foot.
¹⁴Those who love me, I will deliver;
  I will protect those who know my name.
¹⁵When they call to me, I will answer them;
  I will be with them in trouble,
  I will rescue them and honour them.
¹⁶With long life I will satisfy them,
  and show them my salvation.

Notice what this Psalm does *not* say.

It doesn't say you won't be in dangerous places.

It doesn't say you won't be faced with wild and threatening animals.

It doesn't say you won't find yourself in serious trouble.

It says that God will protect you against harm.

It says that you won't need to be afraid of the wild animals, and that you'll be able to trample them underfoot.

It says that God will be with you in trouble, and will rescue you.

It is, in other words, a song with its feet on the ground, even while its heart is praising the living and rescuing God.

It's a good Psalm for Lent, because Lent is a journey that may take us to some difficult and awkward places – in our outward journey of work, family life, church commitments, and other responsibilities, and in our inner journey of moral struggles and spiritual questionings, as we search for God and his ways more deeply than we had before. All these journeys are potentially hard and dangerous, as was Jesus' forty-day fast in the wilderness, with the wild beasts around him and the demons whispering in his ear.

It's at this point that we discover just how dangerous the journey is. Because one of the things the devil whispered in Jesus' ear was a quote from this very Psalm. Perhaps Jesus had memorized it ahead of time and was already using it as a prayer, day by day, to help him through the tough test he was facing. And the devil, seeing he isn't going to succeed by a direct assault on Jesus' senses or appetites, tries a different tack: 'If you really believed this Psalm, then wouldn't you trust God so much that you could throw yourself off the Temple? Doesn't it say he'll send his angels to protect you? Perhaps you don't believe it after all. Perhaps you're just pretending...'

It was actually a bad verse to choose, because the very next line contains the promise that we shall trample the serpent underfoot – which, ever since Genesis 3, had been read as a promise about the coming Child of Eve who would crush the head of the devil himself. Often the right answer to a puzzle in the scriptures, and to the difficulty of praying with them, is to read on, to pray into the wider context and setting, and watch the puzzles resolve and the difficulties recede.

A Psalm for the Lenten journey, then: a prayer that Jesus made his own, and that we can make our own as, with fear and trembling, we set off with him.

Today

Julian of Norwich said, 'Jesus did not say you will not be tempest-tossed. But he did say, "You will not be overcome."' We don't know what we're going to face, but only that God's sheltering care is assured.

Place yourself under his protection. There is no better place to be.

WEEK 1: MONDAY

Luke 2.22–52; focused on 2.22–32

²²When the time came for them to be purified according to the law of Moses, they took him up to Jerusalem to present him before the Lord. ²³That's what the law of the Lord says: 'Every firstborn male shall be called holy to the Lord.' ²⁴They also came

to offer sacrifice, according to what it says in the law of the Lord: 'A pair of turtledoves or two young pigeons.'

[25]Now there was a man in Jerusalem named Simeon. He was righteous and devout, waiting for God to comfort Israel, and the Holy Spirit was upon him. [26]He had been told by the Holy Spirit that he would not die until he had seen the Lord's Messiah. [27]Led by the Spirit, he came into the Temple. As Jesus' parents brought him in, to do for him what the law's regulations required, [28]he took the baby in his arms and blessed God with these words:

[29]'Now, master, you are dismissing your servant in peace,
Just as you said.
[30]These eyes of mine have seen your salvation,
[31]Which you made ready in the presence of all peoples:
[32]A light for revelation to the nations,
And glory for your people Israel.'

Come with me now to the Temple on that spring afternoon. The Temple building itself stands in a much larger open area, itself the size of a small town, with plenty of room for people to come and go, to walk about and meet one another. There are crowds milling about as usual, rich people strolling by with friends and hangers-on, soldiers from the occupying forces looking down from their watchtower, animals and birds being bought and sold in the markets by the gate. There are plenty of beggars about, hoping to cash in on the pilgrims' sense of God's mercy and the obligation to be generous in turn. And there are old people, as always, sitting in the shade, under a tree here and in a doorway there.

Most people don't notice the young couple coming in with their little baby. Happens all the time. No different from countless others. But, as they approach, you see one of the old men get up slowly from his seat. He has a strange look in his eyes. What's he thinking? What's he going to say?

You are almost as alarmed as the parents are when he takes the child from them, but his movement and his embrace is as gentle and firm as the love of God. He has seen something nobody else has. He has been praying and waiting for this moment all his life, and now it's come. This is the Messiah; he's seen him with his own eyes; now he can die in peace.

How do you feel as you hear him say that? What does it make you want to do, or to pray?

Perhaps it makes you simply grateful for the old people you know who have been faithful to God throughout their lives, and who can now go to their graves in peace and gratitude.

Perhaps it challenges you to reflect on what you should be praying for in your lifetime, on the things you long to see happen in God's world, or in your own family, which you will go on waiting and hoping for and trusting that God will let you see.

Perhaps it's more personal: about something in your own life, here and now, which you want to bring to the Temple, into God's presence, for his blessing; something about which you need to hear a word of wisdom and confirmation.

Today

Pray for the Holy Spirit to give you wisdom and inspiration to know what to pray for, and how to recognize God's moment when it comes.

Gracious Lord, give me your Spirit, that I may seek your will and recognize it when it comes.

WEEK 1: TUESDAY
Luke 3; focused on 3.3–6, 10–14

> ³John, the son of Zechariah, went through all the region of the Jordan, announcing a baptism of repentance for the forgiveness

of sins. ⁴This is what is written in the book of the words of Isaiah the prophet:

'A voice shouting in the wilderness:
Get ready a path for the Lord,
Make the roads straight for him!
⁵Every valley shall be filled in,
And every mountain and hill shall be flattened,
The twisted paths will be straightened out,
And the rough roads smoothed off,
⁶And all that lives shall see God's rescue.'

¹⁰'What shall we do?' asked the crowds.

¹¹'Anyone who has two cloaks,' replied John, 'should give one to someone who hasn't got one. The same applies to anyone who has plenty of food.'

¹²Some toll-collectors came to be baptized. 'Teacher,' they said, 'what should we do?'

¹³'Don't collect more than what is laid down,' he replied.

¹⁴Some soldiers, too, asked John, 'What about us? What should we do?'

'No extortion,' replied John, 'and no blackmail. Be content with your wages.'

Come down now to the lowest point on the face of the earth. When you drive from Jerusalem into the Jordan valley, roughly halfway down the road you pass a sign saying 'Sea Level'. If you'd been going in the other direction you would now be standing by the Mediterranean Sea. Instead, you've still got a long way to go, down into the valley that ends with the Dead Sea. You can't get lower than that without digging a tunnel.

John the Baptist knew he had a job to do, and we as spectators gather round, listening to his stirring talk and seeing how people react. He had come to the lowest point on earth because that was where God had met with his people before when they were on the verge of crossing over into the promised land. John believes that God's people now are on the verge of something new, something even bigger.

We join the crowds as they press round him. We hear his grand description of the new things that are going to happen. It's like Isaiah said! God is going to flatten the hills and fill in the valleys, because he is coming back to his people in person, back to his world, and he's going to straighten everything out! The whole world needs to roll out the red carpet to greet him when he comes.

Stirring talk, and as we listen we think to ourselves, 'Yes! There's so much in the world that needs straightening out!' There's terrorism, famine, war and all kinds of bitterness. Even around where I live people are unhappy, or unemployed, or unloved. Or all three. We want God to come back and sort it all out. And we start to pray that it may be so indeed.

As we read further on in the story we discover just how God is coming back. It won't look like a pillar of fire, or a chariot with whirling wheels. It will look like... Jesus.

How Jesus will sort everything out remains to be seen as Luke's story unfolds. What we discover at this point is that the sorting-out process begins here and now. We've come to hear about the big picture, about the whole world being put to rights. But we are brought down to earth with a bump by the questions people are asking and the answers they're receiving. People ask: 'What should we do?' Answer: 'Straighten your lives out in the simplest, most direct way.'

Today

Most of us know the places where, in our own lives, there are mountains to be flattened and valleys to be filled in, if God is to come and take up residence.

Lord, show me how my life can be straightened out, so that your healing, restoring power may flow through me to the world around.

15

WEEK 1: WEDNESDAY
Luke 4; focused on 4.14–30

[14]Jesus returned to Galilee in the power of the Spirit. Word about him went out throughout the whole district. [15]He taught in their synagogues, and gained a great reputation all around.

[16]He came to Nazareth, where he had been brought up. On the sabbath, as was his regular practice, he went in to the synagogue and stood up to read. [17]They gave him the scroll of the prophet Isaiah. He unrolled the scroll and found the place where it was written:

[18]'The Spirit of the Lord is upon me
Because he has anointed me
To tell the poor the good news.
He has sent me to announce release to the prisoners
And sight to the blind,
To set the wounded victims free,
[19]To announce the year of God's special favour.'

[20]He rolled up the scroll, gave it to the attendant, and sat down. All eyes in the synagogue were fixed on him.

[21]'Today,' he began, 'this scripture is fulfilled in your own hearing.'

[22]Everyone remarked at him; they were astonished at the words coming out of his mouth – words of sheer grace.

'Isn't this Joseph's son?' they said.

[23]'I know what you're going to say,' Jesus said. 'You're going to tell me the old riddle: "Heal yourself, doctor!" "We heard of great happenings in Capernaum; do things like that here, in your own country!"

[24]'Let me tell you the truth,' he went on. 'Prophets never get accepted in their own country. [25]This is the solemn truth: there were plenty of widows in Israel in the time of Elijah, when heaven was shut up for three years and six months, and there was a great famine over all the land. [26]Elijah was sent to none of them, only to a widow in the Sidonian town of Zarephath.

²⁷'And there were plenty of people with virulent skin diseases in Israel in the time of Elisha the prophet, and none of them were healed – only Naaman, the Syrian.'

²⁸When they heard this, everyone in the synagogue flew into a rage. ²⁹They got up and threw him out of town. They took him to the top of the mountain on which the town was built, meaning to fling him off. ³⁰But he slipped through the middle of them and went away.

'Everyone wants to serve God,' declared the poster outside the church, 'but only in an advisory capacity.' We all know what we want God to do. We are not so good at bringing our hopes and intentions into line with what God has in mind.

This was never more graphically illustrated than when Jesus, having begun his work of launching God's kingdom elsewhere, came back to his home town. Not only did everybody know him and his family (always a tricky situation), they knew what, if he really was bringing God's kingdom, he ought to be doing.

Imagine yourself that sabbath morning, standing at the back of the synagogue with this young man, apparently some kind of a prophet, sitting down in the teacher's chair. (As a teacher I've always rather liked the idea of sitting down and having the audience stand up, but I doubt it would catch on these days.) The main thing you know is that you and your people are in a big mess, and it's time God sorted it out. Anyone claiming to be a prophet – let alone quoting the scriptures and saying they're all coming true – ought to be telling us how God will rescue his own poor people, sort out the bad characters, and smash the heathen invaders to smithereens. That is how it's supposed to work. That is what God is meant to be doing!

But look at what happens next. This young would-be prophet is talking about *grace* – about 'the year of God's favour'. Well, that's fine; we know about the Jubilee, the time when everyone is to be released from all their debts. Maybe it's time we did it once for all, and more thoroughly. But…he's talking about God doing it for *everybody*! The wicked and the pagans are going to be let off as well! We can't have that! Who does he think he is? He deserves to be lynched!

Are you angry? You should be. He's just stood all your good, sound advice on its head. Unfortunately, God tends to do that; Jesus himself tended to do that. God is turning the whole world upside down. That means he's turning *your* whole world upside down as well.

Today

As we allow a scene like this to wash over us, we will sometimes hear the disturbing question: when we know, only too clearly, what God ought to be doing, are we prepared to take a second opinion? God's opinion?

Sovereign Lord, teach me to listen to you even when you're saying things I badly don't want to hear.

WEEK 1: THURSDAY
Luke 5; focused on 5.1–11

¹One day, as the crowds were pressing close to him to hear the word of God, Jesus was standing by the lake of Gennesaret. ²He saw two boats moored by the land; the fishermen had gone ashore and were washing their nets. ³He got into one of the boats – it was Simon's – and asked him to put out a little way from the land. Then he sat down in the boat and began to teach the crowd.

⁴When he had finished speaking, he said to Simon, 'Put out into the deeper part, and let down your nets for a catch.'

⁵'Master,' replied Simon, 'we were working hard all night and caught nothing at all. But if you say so, I'll let down the nets.'

⁶When they did so, they caught such a huge number of fish that their nets began to break. ⁷They signalled to their partners

in the other boat to come and help them. So they came, and filled both the boats, and they began to sink.

⁸When Simon Peter saw it, he fell down at Jesus' knees.

'Go away,' he said. 'Leave me, Lord! I'm a sinner!' ⁹He and all his companions were gripped with amazement at the catch of fish they had taken; ¹⁰this included James and John, the sons of Zebedee, who were partners with Simon.

'Don't be afraid,' said Jesus to Simon. 'From now on you'll be catching people.'

¹¹They brought the boats in to land. Then they abandoned everything and followed him.

So there you are, going about your ordinary everyday business, and one day someone comes up to you. You've seen him before, around the place. But, frankly, times are tough; you're busy. Prophets and God-botherers have been coming and going all your life and so far nothing much has changed.

So when he tells you he's going to borrow your boat, well, it's a bit of a nuisance, but you shrug your shoulders and help him to get out into the bay where the crowds can hear. (That part of the shoreline is dotted with little bays that form natural amphitheatres.) You're minding the boat as it rests at anchor but you can't help listening to what he's saying. He's talking about God becoming king, about everything being different, about a new day dawning in which the poor are going to be helped up out of the mud. Well, if he could change a few things around here he'd be most welcome to try, but frankly we're not holding out that much hope.

Ah, now he's finishing. Back to the shore, I guess. He'll be on to another village. Actually, I'm ready for bed. It's been a long night out on the lake and nothing to show for it ...

But what's this? He says he wants us to go fishing again! What's that about? Doesn't he know that night-time is when the fish gather? Is he crazy or what? But something about the way he says it makes you do it anyway ...

And the next thing you know, it isn't just the fish that are caught…it's you! He seems to know something that goes deeper than everything else. He seems to have a purpose, a plan. He wants helpers. Why me? Goodness knows, but actually (I know it sounds a bit stupid) there's something about him I've never seen before. Maybe this is for real. Maybe *he* is for real. Maybe he thinks *I'm* for real. That's a scary thought. In fact (it just strikes me), if he's really a prophet, and if he wants me to work with him, my life might have to change. Just a bit. Don't think I want that…

But what's that? He's laughing. 'Get up, Peter. You're going to be catching people from now on.'

What? You mean me? You can't be serious, Lord. But he is. Very serious. But also very light-touch. Come on, Peter. This is the first day of the rest of your life.

Today

Lord, help me to hear your call and be ready to respond. I'm not perfect but I'm ready to have you take charge.

WEEK 1: FRIDAY
Luke 6; focused on 6.20–27

²⁰He lifted up his eyes and looked at his disciples, and said:

> 'Blessings on the poor: God's kingdom belongs to you!
> ²¹'Blessings on those who are hungry today: you'll have a feast!
> 'Blessings on those who weep today: you'll be laughing!
> ²²'Blessings on you, when people hate you, and shut you out, when they slander you and reject your name as if it was evil, because of the son of man. ²³Celebrate on that day! Jump for joy! Don't you see: in heaven there is a great reward for you! That's what their ancestors did to the prophets.

> ²⁴'But woe betide you rich: you've had your comfort!
> ²⁵'Woe betide you if you're full today: you'll go hungry!
> ²⁶'Woe betide you if you're laughing today: you'll be mourning and weeping!
> ²⁷'Woe betide you when everyone speaks well of you: that's what their ancestors did to the false prophets.'

How old were you when you first learned some nursery rhymes?

Probably quite young. In fact, many children can sing a few rhymes long before they understand what half the words mean. It's a great way for kids to start learning things, exercising their young brains with music and words and rhythm and rhyme. It's the equivalent of learning how to ride on a swing or how to do a little dance.

Now supposing you were in the crowd listening to Jesus telling you all kinds of things about God and his kingdom. So much to take in, so much to think through, so much to try to remember...but wait, he's teaching us something, something we can learn quite easily. It goes with a swing and a flow.

'Blessings on the poor; blessings on the hungry; blessings on the weeping, blessings when they hate you. Woe betide the rich, woe betide the full, woe betide the laughing, woe betide the popular!' *Now, repeat after me*...and soon the whole crowd is joining in. (To the confusion of some who've come from the next town where Jesus taught them a slightly different version of the same thing. He seems to develop it as he goes along.)

But what does it all *mean*? Well, we're working on that. It's a bit like the words they say his mother sang when she knew he was on the way: the rich getting brought down with a bump and the poor getting a leg up. God turning the world the right way up at last. Promises, promises...but it does seem to be coming true, for some people at least. That old lady down the road, the fisherman's mother, looks twenty years younger since he prayed for her when she was ill the other day. And as for that poor young man with the withered arm – well, I don't care what day of the week it was, anyone who can cure someone like that gets my vote. And they say if you get near enough to him in the crowd you can sense a kind of healing aura all around him. So if he's saying that the world is being sorted out, straightened out, at last, maybe it's true.

But not everybody's going to like it. There are already mutterings and mumblings in the background. After all, that's what you'd expect, going around teaching people rhymes like that. Wonder how long he'll survive if he keeps this up – the occupying forces have eyes and ears everywhere, and old Happy Herod up the road isn't going to be exactly jumping for joy either.

In fact, maybe that's what the rhyme means. Maybe it's not just a general truth we have to learn. Maybe we need to think out who Jesus actually has in mind...

Today

Read again slowly the words in verses 20–23.

Lord, help me to learn your new song, and to find out what it means in our world today.

WEEK 1: SATURDAY

Luke 13.31–35

[31]Just then some Pharisees came up and spoke to Jesus.

'Get away from here,' they said, 'because Herod wants to kill you.'

[32]'Go and tell that fox,' replied Jesus, ' "Look here: I'm casting out demons today and tomorrow, and completing my healings. I'll be finished by the third day. [33]But I have to continue my travels today, tomorrow and the day after that! It couldn't happen that a prophet would perish anywhere except Jerusalem."

³⁴'Jerusalem, Jerusalem! You kill the prophets, and stone the people sent to you! How many times did I want to collect your children, like a hen gathers her brood under her wings, and you would have none of it! ³⁵Look, your house has been abandoned. Let me tell you this: you will never see me until you are prepared to say, "A blessing upon you! Welcome in the name of the Lord!"'

There they stood, on the television news the other night. A family huddled together, staring at the charred remains of what, twelve hours before, had been their home. The forest fires had swept through that part of the country and they, like many others, had lost everything except what they stood up in. It's one of the most horrifying things that can happen to a family. And of course if you and your children are caught up in it the only thing you really care about is making sure they all get out safely.

That instinct of preserving the children runs through the animal kingdom as well. In fact, what Jesus is saying here would have rung bells with his hearers at that level. 'How many times did I want to collect your children, like a hen gathers her brood under her wings.' When the fire comes raging through the farmyard, the hen gathers the chicks under her wings, and sometimes when the fire is over you will find the moving sight of a dead hen, charred and blackened with the fire and smoke, but with live chicks still huddled under her wings. The mother hen has, quite literally, given her life to save her children.

So, what is Jesus saying here, and how can we begin to understand what it means for us?

Perhaps we're with Jesus and his party as those Pharisees (friendly ones, as occasionally they are in Luke) come to warn him that Herod, the local king who doesn't like rival 'kings' on his patch, is out to get him. You can feel the tension in the air.

Some of us knew it might end in this way; all the talk about the rich and the powerful being thrown down and the poor and humble raised up was bound to lead to trouble, however much it's in the Bible! Now what shall we do? Now what will *he* do?

Our natural instinct is to say, 'Come on, Jesus, you've made your point; now it's time to move on, to go somewhere safer.' But what's he saying? 'No; Herod can't touch me; prophets die in Jerusalem. Didn't you know that?'

That's extraordinary! And scary. Surely he doesn't mean he's going to Jerusalem ... in order to *die* there?

'Jerusalem, Jerusalem!' Think of the hen and the chicks. Think of the fire that will sweep through the farmyard. Yes, I'm coming to Jerusalem, and that's what I wanted to do for all of you, to take the fire on myself, the fire of Herod, the fire of Rome, the fire of all the wickedness in the world. But are you going to be ready for it? Or will you reject your one chance of safety?

Today

Lord, we don't always understand what you're up to, or why you went to die in that way. But we pray for strength to follow wherever you go, to be sheltered under your wings from all the evil that may come.

WEEK 2: SUNDAY

Psalm 27

¹The Lord is my light and my salvation; whom shall I fear?
   The Lord is the stronghold of my life; of whom shall I be afraid?
²When evildoers assail me to devour my flesh – my enemies and foes –
   they shall stumble and fall.
³Though an army encamp against me, my heart shall not fear;
   though war rise up against me, yet will I be confident.

⁴One thing I asked of the Lord, that will I seek after:
    to live in the house of the Lord all the days of my life,
    to behold the beauty of the Lord,
    and to inquire in his temple.
⁵For he will hide me in his shelter in the day of trouble;
    he will conceal me under the cover of his tent;
    he will set me high on a rock.
⁶Now my head is lifted up above my enemies all around me,
    and I will offer in his tent sacrifices with shouts of joy;
    I will sing and make melody to the Lord.
⁷Hear, O Lord, when I cry aloud,
    be gracious to me and answer me!
⁸'Come,' my heart says, 'seek his face!'
    Your face, Lord, do I seek.
⁹Do not hide your face from me.
    Do not turn your servant away in anger,
    you who have been my help.
    Do not cast me off, do not forsake me,
    O God of my salvation!
¹⁰If my father and mother forsake me,
    the Lord will take me up.
¹¹Teach me your way, O Lord,
    and lead me on a level path because of my enemies.
¹²Do not give me up to the will of my adversaries,
    for false witnesses have risen against me,
    and they are breathing out violence.
¹³I believe that I shall see the goodness of the Lord
    in the land of the living.
¹⁴Wait for the Lord;
    be strong, and let your heart take courage;
    wait for the Lord!

Look for him and wait for him.

Those are the two key Lenten messages that come out of this Psalm. 'Come on,' the Psalmist says to his own heart, 'seek his face!'

Isn't this strange? Isn't God always available? Why do we have to work hard at looking for him?

God is gracious, and longs to be found by people of all sorts and at all times. But God does not put himself about as a mere item of curiosity, a show for the spiritual tourists, so that anyone can pop in and glance at him, shrug their shoulders and walk away. You have to want to go looking for him, so that when you find him and know you're in his presence it's a thing of awe and joy and wonder, a demanding and challenging but also warming and healing presence that gives you the strength you need.

And looking for him takes time. You have to *wait* as well as look.

We are familiar with the story of the eager European explorer setting off into the African bush, followed by Africans carrying his baggage. After two or three days the followers refuse to go any further for a while. They aren't tired, they explain. They are waiting for their souls to catch up.

Well, I think God is a bit like that. We want results *now*. A recent advertisement for a new mobile phone shouts that 'Impatience is a Virtue!' It isn't. It's a vice. A damaging one to human relationships, and still more damaging to our relationship with God.

Looking for God and waiting for God are important not least because we are surrounded by enemies. That may sound almost paranoid. We want to ask the Psalmist: 'Who are these "enemies"? What's the problem? Why don't you thank God for your friends instead of worrying about people being out to get you?'

Part of the answer is that David, the original Psalmist, spent much of his life surrounded by all sorts of enemies – Philistines, Saul and his followers, other foreign nations and then, darkly, enemies within his own family. But David's experience acts as a signpost to the fact that anyone who wants to seek God and wait for him will face struggles of various kinds. Sometimes other people will resent what you're doing, or criticize you. Even in our supposedly 'free society' some people so hate the Christian message that they make it impossible for Christians to hold down particular jobs.

Then there are the other enemies: the accusing and wheedling and mocking voices within our own heads and hearts. These often become just that bit louder when, in Lent and at similar times, we set ourselves to seek God and to wait for him.

Today

This is the Psalm you need when those voices start to become threatening, and you need to remind yourself where your real stronghold lies.

Lord, be my light and my salvation, today, this week, and for ever.

WEEK 2: MONDAY
Luke 7.1–17; focused on 7.11–17

[11]Not long afterwards, Jesus went to a town called Nain. His disciples went with him, and so did a large crowd. [12]As he got near to the gate of the city, a young man was being carried out dead. He was the only son of his mother, and she was a widow. There was a substantial crowd of the townspeople with her.

[13]When the Master saw her, he was very sorry for her. 'Don't cry,' he said to her. [14]Then he went up and touched the bier, and the people carrying it stood still.

'Young fellow,' he said, 'I'm telling you – get up!' [15]The dead man sat up and began to speak, and he gave him to his mother.

[16]Terror came over all of them. They praised God.

'A great prophet has risen among us!' they said. 'God has visited his people!'

[17]This report went out about him in the whole of Judaea and the surrounding countryside.

How good are you at wailing?

In many countries in the world to this day, people attending funerals (especially the women) are expected to weep and wail and make as much noise as they can.

Most people in the West don't do that kind of mourning. But supposing you're there, in the crowd, that day at Nain. The dead man was the last best hope of his mother. In the days before social security benefits, and before most women could earn a living wage all by themselves, a widow depended on her son to look after her. And now he's gone.

The whole village has turned out to grieve with her, to help her express, in that heart-rending fashion, the sorrow and fear that now seem to wrap themselves round her and cling to her like a cold, wet cloak.

As you are walking slowly along, to the burial-place outside the city, you're aware of a change in the mood over the other side of the crowd. It's that prophet and his followers, the ones who've been going around saying that it's time for God to become king! Not sure we want folk like that around here, and this is hardly the moment for a political rally...

But what's he doing? He's coming up to the...to the dead man! What's he going to do now? He should know you can't touch dead bodies. It'll make him unclean. Surely he knows that!...

And then it happens. Jesus doesn't just touch the dead man. He speaks to him. Tells him in no uncertain terms to get up, like a parent telling a sulky child it's time to wake up and get off to school. What does he think he's doing?

And then...Terror. Amazement. Fear. Tingles down the spine. The funeral wailing stops in its tracks and changes to the sort of celebration-noises people make at a wedding. He's alive! He's getting up! Jesus is smiling and laughing and handing him to his mother. She can't believe it. She doesn't know whether to laugh or cry or faint. She just hugs her son and then hugs Jesus, and it's laughter and hugs all round while the procession disperses with more of a buzz than fifty beehives put together.

What's happening? God has come to rescue his people! God has raised up a prophet! It's all true! God is becoming king!

But then Jesus, making his way back through the crowd, stops beside you. You half wanted this, but were half afraid of it too. What's he going to say?

Today

Pause, and think, and listen. He has a particular word for you today. You can turn away, if you like, and pretend he isn't talking to you. But you might be far better listening to what he says. Then think and pray about what it means for his life-giving kingdom to come into your village, your family, your life.

WEEK 2: TUESDAY

Luke 7.18–50; focused on 7.18–28

[18]The disciples of John the Baptist told him about all these things. John called two of these followers [19]and sent them to the Master with this message: 'Are you the Coming One, or should we expect someone else?'

[20]The men arrived where Jesus was. 'John the Baptist', they said, 'has sent us to you to say, "Are you the Coming One, or should we expect someone else?"'

[21]Then and there Jesus healed several people of diseases, plagues and possession by unclean spirits; and he gave several blind people back their sight. [22]Then he answered them:

'Go and tell John what you have seen and heard: The blind see, the lame walk, people with virulent skin diseases are cleansed, the deaf hear, the dead are raised, the poor hear the gospel. [23]And a blessing on the person who isn't shocked by me!'

[24]So off went John's messengers.

Jesus then began to talk to the crowds about John.

'Why did you go out into the desert?' he asked. 'What were you looking for? A reed swaying in the breeze? [25]Well then, what did you go out to see? Someone dressed in silks and satins? See here, if you want to find people who wear fine clothes and live in luxury, you'd better look in royal palaces. [26]So what did you go out to see? A prophet? Yes indeed, and more than a prophet. [27]This is the one of whom the Bible says, "Look: I send my messenger before my face; he will get my path ready ahead of me."

[28]'Let me tell you this:' he went on; 'nobody greater than John has ever been born of women. But the one who is least in God's kingdom is greater than he is.'

If you've seen a politician being interviewed on the television, you know how it goes. The interviewer presses home the questions, and the politician says something different. Changes the subject. Never gives a straight answer. They wriggle and squirm, because they know if they say it straight it'll be all over the papers the next day.

'Would you say,' asks the interviewer, 'that the party leaders were having a difficult time right now?' 'Well, yes,' says the young and nervous politician, because that is actually the truth. Next day the headlines scream, '"My Leader In Difficulties" says New MP'. Actually, he didn't say that. He certainly didn't volunteer it. The journalist put words into his mouth.

Jesus faced exactly the same problem, and it will help us understand the kind of conversation we have here if we imagine people standing around waiting for Jesus to say something that, whispered to the authorities, will get him into trouble.

So he answers the question not by *saying* something but by *doing* something; doing, in fact, what the Bible said the Messiah would do when he came: open blind eyes, unstop deaf ears, even raise the dead. 'Draw your own conclusions,' he seems to be saying. 'And think about this: God's blessing will fall on those who are not shocked by me, not ashamed of the fact that I'm not exactly what they were expecting.'

Then Jesus asks a question in his turn. 'When you went out to see John the Baptist, what were you looking for? A king, in the ordinary sense? [Herod had had the Galilean reed stamped on his coins, so "a reed shaken in the wind" was a way of saying "someone like old what's-his-name up the road".] No: you've had enough royals and celebrities with their fancy ways to last you a lifetime. No – what you wanted was a prophet. Someone who would announce that God was coming to put everything right at last. And you were right, because that's exactly what John was.'

So far, so good. Jesus appears to be talking about John. But then we realize, listening closely, that he is talking about himself and his work as well, but still in a way that won't allow any spies listening in to get any hard evidence of what he is really claiming. 'John was the greatest mother's son ever,' he says; 'but anyone inside God's kingdom is greater still.' In other words, for those with ears to hear, Jesus is claiming that he is indeed the One Who Was Coming, the one who would change everything. That's a dangerous claim today, as it was then.

Today

Try to be quiet for a moment and think about Jesus saying to you, 'And a blessing on the person who isn't shocked by me!'

Does Jesus shock you in what he says or does? Talk to him about that.

Lord, give me the courage to understand what you really want to do for the world, for my community and for me.

WEEK 2: WEDNESDAY

Luke 8.1–39; focused on 8.22–39

22One day he got into a boat with his disciples, and suggested that they cross to the other shore. So they set off. 23As they were

31

sailing, he fell asleep. A violent wind swept down on the lake, and the boat began to fill dangerously with water.

²⁴'Master, Master!' shouted the disciples, coming and waking him up. 'Master, we're lost!'

He got up and scolded the wind and the waves. They stopped, and there was a flat calm.

²⁵'Where's your faith?' he asked them.

They were afraid and astonished. 'Who is this, then,' they asked one another, 'if he can give orders to wind and water, and they obey him?'

²⁶They sailed to the land of the Gerasenes, which is on the other side from Galilee. ²⁷As he got out on land, a demon-possessed man from the town met him. For a long time he had worn no clothes, and he didn't live in a house but among the tombs. ²⁸When he saw Jesus he screamed and fell down in front of him.

'You and me, Jesus – you and me!' he yelled at the top of his voice. 'What is it with you and me, you son of the Most High God? Don't torture me – please, please don't torment me!' ²⁹Jesus was commanding the unclean spirit to come out of the man. Many times over it had seized him, and he was kept under guard with chains and manacles; but he used to break the shackles, and the demon would drive him into the desert.

³⁰'What's your name?' Jesus asked him.

'Regiment!' replied the man – for many demons had entered him. ³¹And they begged him not to order them to be sent into the Pit.

³²A sizeable herd of pigs was feeding on the hillside, and they begged him to allow them to go into them. He gave them permission. ³³The demons went out of the man and entered the pigs, and the herd rushed down the steep slope into the lake and was drowned.

³⁴The herdsmen saw what had happened. They took to their heels and spread the news in town and country, ³⁵and people came out to see what had happened. They came to Jesus, and found the man from whom the demons had gone out sitting there at Jesus' feet, clothed and in his right mind. They were

afraid. [36]People who had seen how the demoniac had been healed explained it to them. [37]The whole crowd, from the surrounding country of the Gerasenes, asked him to go away from them, because great terror had seized them. So he got into the boat and returned.

[38]The man who had been demon-possessed begged Jesus to let him stay with him. But he sent him away. [39]'Go back to your home,' he said, 'and tell them what God has done for you.' And he went off round every town, declaring what Jesus had done for him.

How do you pray inside a story like that?

It's easy enough to imagine yourself on that little boat, tossed this way and that by the sudden storm that sweeps down on the lake. Some may even have experienced a storm like that, and those who haven't can imagine it, or use it as a picture for the times when life is troubled and turbulent, with disasters, horror stories, tragedies and personal anxieties bearing down on us like ten-foot waves.

At times like that there is no shame in praying 'Master, we're lost.' If it seems like Jesus is asleep, then wake him up. That's what the Psalms do, after all: 'Wake up, God! Why are you asleep? Something needs doing around here!' If you believe in a living God, use a little holy boldness.

Jesus both answers their request and inquires ruefully about their panicky lack of faith. 'What came over you? Didn't you trust me?' Answer: 'Well, we did, or we wouldn't have woken you up; but I guess we didn't, or we wouldn't have panicked.' That seems to me a fair position for a follower of Jesus to be in.

But the second half of the story – and Luke, as he often does, puts things together because they make a natural set – is harder again. Most of us haven't had much to do with demon-possession, and probably don't want to. People who know about these things will assure us that there is a dark, sad reality behind this language, even if we can't fit it into today's scientific categories. Just because some people go to the other extreme and imagine demons hiding behind every bush, that doesn't mean there isn't a realm of spiritual activity that can only accurately be described in something like those terms.

In this instance – and there are reported cases like this today as well – it seems that the poor man in the middle of the story was overwhelmed from within by what he calls 'Regiment' – the Roman 'legion', a troop of four or five thousand soldiers, well equipped, professionally trained killers. Some have speculated that his condition had been brought on by the trauma of seeing soldiers trampling through his country, polluting it with their pagan ways, crushing rebellions with casual brutality.

So how do you pray inside a story like *that*?

Today

Sit with the scene in front of you for a while and pray for all those who, today, see violence sweeping through their village or their region.

Pray for all those whose anger and fear have turned in on themselves until they have forgotten who they are and can only think of the terrible enemy.

Pray for the power of Jesus to dispel the demons, whatever they are, that grip so many people in anger and fear.

Ask for wisdom to look into the depths of your own heart and tell Jesus what names are haunting you just now.

WEEK 2: THURSDAY

Luke 8.40–56

[40]Jesus returned. A large crowd was waiting for him, and welcomed him back. [41]A man named Jairus, a ruler of the synagogue, came and fell down in front of his feet. He pleaded with him to come

to his house, [42]because he had an only daughter, twelve years old, who was dying. So they set off, and the crowd pressed close in around him.

[43]There was a woman who had had an internal haemorrhage for twelve years. She had spent all she had on doctors, but had not been able to find a cure from anyone. [44]She came up behind Jesus and touched the hem of his robe. Immediately her flow of blood dried up.

[45]'Who touched me?' asked Jesus.

Everybody denied it. 'Master,' said Peter, 'the crowds are crushing you and pressing you!'

[46]'Somebody touched me,' said Jesus. 'Power went out from me, and I knew it.'

[47]When the woman saw that she couldn't remain hidden, she came up, trembling, and fell down in front of him. She told him, in front of everyone, why she had touched him, and how she had been healed instantly.

[48]'Daughter,' said Jesus, 'your faith has saved you. Go in peace.'

[49]While he was still speaking, someone arrived from the synagogue-ruler's house. 'Your daughter's dead,' he said. 'Don't bother the teacher any longer.'

[50]'Don't be afraid,' said Jesus when he heard it. 'Just believe, and she will be rescued.'

[51]When they got to the house, he didn't let anyone come in with them except Peter, John and James, and the child's father and mother. [52]Everyone was weeping and wailing for her.

'Don't cry,' said Jesus, 'she isn't dead; she's asleep.' [53]They laughed at him, knowing that she was dead.

[54]But he took her by the hand. 'Get up, child,' he called. [55]Her spirit returned, and she got up at once. He told them to give her something to eat. [56]Her parents were astounded, but he told them to tell nobody what had happened.

Another double story. This one may be easier to live inside and make our own. We in the modern Western world are used to comparatively sedate behaviour and crowd control, but there was nothing sedate or controlled about people when Jesus was around. We have to imagine a seething, pushing crowd, like people spilling out of a football ground or like shoppers at the beginning of a great sale. Everyone wants to get close to where they think the action is. Here you are, in the middle of that crowd, a bit nervous of being pushed off your feet, but determined to get close to Jesus if you can.

Then, suddenly, he wheels round and asks a question.

'Who touched me?'

Well, you think, I wish it had been me, because I was trying to get close enough…but his followers are protesting, shaking their heads at him, shrugging their shoulders. 'What d'you mean, who touched you? Everyone's touching you! What part of "this is a crowd" don't you understand?'

'No,' says Jesus, 'I want to know who touched me. *I felt power go out from me.*'

That is the point in the story, or rather the first point in the story, where we ought to pause and pray. Even those of us who've been Christians for many years find it easy to lapse back into thinking of Jesus as basically just another great teacher, even as the one who died for us; but the thought that he had that kind of power, and was conscious of it going out from him…that's hard to imagine. But worth pondering, because it's still true and you never know when you are going to need it. Better to stay close to him all the time…

So the woman comes and confesses. She had been afraid because, with her ailment, she was 'unclean', and she must have known that by pushing through the crowd like that she'd made everyone she'd touched 'unclean' as well. Particularly Jesus. But with Jesus it didn't work like that. Here's the thing, the point at which our prayers should be focused. By ordinary rules, we should make *him* unclean, pressing upon him with our messy and muddled lives. But when we come to him in faith, it works the other way. His power makes us clean again. That's near the very heart of the gospel.

Come in faith! That's the challenge all through. We go with Jesus to Jairus' house. We hear the servants saying there's no point, the little girl is dead. We wait outside the door as Jesus goes in. And then it happens again. Power and glory. New life.

Today

'Don't be afraid,' Jesus had said. 'Just believe.'

Is this the moment to stop in your tracks, to face your fears and give them to Jesus? Trust him, and his power can and will bring new life where it's needed.

WEEK 2: FRIDAY

Luke 9.1–36; focused on 9.18–27

[18]When Jesus was praying alone, his disciples gathered around him.

'Who do the crowds say I am?' he asked them.

[19]'John the Baptist,' they responded. 'And others say Elijah. Others say that one of the ancient prophets has arisen.'

[20]'What about you?' said Jesus. 'Who do you say I am?'

'God's Messiah,' answered Peter.

[21]He gave them strict and careful instructions not to tell this to anyone.

[22]'The son of man,' he said, 'must suffer many things, and be rejected by the elders, and the chief priests, and the legal experts. He must be killed, and raised up on the third day.'

[23]He then spoke to them all. 'If any of you want to come after me,' he said, 'you must say No to yourselves, and pick up your cross every day, and follow me. [24]If you want to save your life, you'll lose it; but if you lose your life because of me, you'll save it. [25]What good will it do you if you win the entire world, but lose or forfeit your own self? [26]If you're ashamed of me and my words, the son of man will be ashamed of you, when he comes

in the glory which belongs to him, and to his father, and to the holy angels.

[27]'Let me tell you,' he concluded, 'there are some standing here who won't experience death until they see God's kingdom.'

Everybody, it seems, loves a TV quiz. Sometimes the contestants get it right, and come out smiling. Other times, they either forget something they know perfectly well or reveal that they didn't know as much as they had hoped they did.

But at least the only things that hang on their getting the right answer are the prize and the glow of satisfaction.

But there are some questions that, depending on your answer, will change your life for ever.

'Is this the path we should take to get down the mountain?' Get the answer wrong and you could be heading for disaster.

'Is this the person I should marry?' Get that one wrong – either way – and you face lasting unhappiness.

And so on.

Jesus' question about who his followers thought he was is a question like that. It wasn't just a quiz, sitting round the campfire one night and seeing what people think, but then going on much as before. He needed to know that they had got the message, that they had worked it out.

It wasn't an easy question, because 'God's Messiah' was supposed to do various things that Jesus hadn't done. The coming Messiah, the 'anointed king', was supposed to rebuild the Temple in Jerusalem. He was supposed to defeat the enemy armies, the pagans. And he was supposed to bring justice and peace to the world by establishing a new rule, a new way of governing God's people and God's world. And though Jesus had done many remarkable things he hadn't actually done any of those.

What would you say, sitting round the fire with his followers?

You might play safe, and agree with the people they quoted. 'People say you're a prophet, like one of the great ones we've read about in the Bible.'

Or are you ready to take a deep breath and blurt out the conclusion that Peter and the others were coming to? 'You're God's Messiah!' You're the King, the Coming One. You're not just a prophet. You're the one we've been waiting for!

That answer has immediate consequences. If you think Jesus is the Messiah, then you are committed to following him, even when he tells you he's off to the big city to die. This wasn't just a quiz.

Are you ready for that? Many people today, even many Christians, really do believe that the point of life is 'to be true to yourself' or 'to find out who you really are' and then try to live like that. Jesus stands all that on its head. 'If you want to gain your life, you have to lose it.'

Today

Imagine that you are sitting around the fire and listen to Jesus asking you, 'Who do you say I am?' Tell him your answer.

Tell him how much you love him, and what things you find difficult.

Ask him to give you a share in his courage, to follow him wherever he leads and whatever it costs.

WEEK 2: SATURDAY

Luke 13.1–9

[1]At that moment some people came up and told them the news. Some Galileans had been in the Temple, and Pilate had mixed their blood with that of the sacrifices.

[2]'Do you suppose', said Jesus, 'that those Galileans suffered such things because they were greater sinners than all other Galileans? [3]No, let me tell you! Unless you repent, you will all be destroyed in the same way.

⁴'And what about those eighteen who were killed when the tower in Siloam collapsed on top of them? Do you imagine they were more blameworthy than everyone else who lives in Jerusalem? ⁵No, let me tell you! Unless you repent, you will all be destroyed in the same way.'

⁶He told them this parable. 'Once upon a time there was a man who had a fig tree in his vineyard. He came to it looking for fruit, and didn't find any. ⁷So he said to the gardener, "Look here! I've been coming to this fig tree for three years hoping to find some fruit, and I haven't found any! Cut it down! Why should it use up the soil?"

⁸"I tell you what, master," replied the gardener; "let it alone for just this one year more. I'll dig all round it and put on some manure. ⁹Then, if it fruits next year, well and good; and if not, you can cut it down."'

Standing in the crowd, you may well want to put your hands over your ears. These are some of the most ferocious words Jesus is recorded as having spoken. Two horrendous incidents – one, a bit of classic Roman brutality, a sort of state-sponsored terrorism; the other, a horrific disaster with people killed by a falling building. You'd expect Jesus to be sympathetic! Surely, you think, he's lost it this time. What can he be talking about? 'Unless you repent, you'll all perish in the same way!' Whatever does this mean?

Then, as the crowd murmurs in dismay and people look at one another, frightened and horrified, you begin to put it together. Jesus has been talking about God turning the world upside down. He has been doing things that have forced you and your friends to conclude that he really is the Messiah, even though he's not doing the specific things you thought a Messiah would. And in and through all his teaching there has been a strange and dark note: that he has indeed come to rescue God's people, but that there will be many people who won't want to be rescued, or not by him, or not in that way. What on earth will happen next?

Jesus' warnings are now very stark and specific. They have been already, and they will stay that way. If you follow him, you'll hear more in the same vein. And the point is this. Jesus isn't being vindictive or hostile. He doesn't want to see people's lives destroyed. *He is acting like a fire officer trying to wake up people who are deep in a drugged sleep in a building whose lower floors are already ablaze.* 'If you don't get up, you're all dead!' Saying that – yelling it at the sleeping forms – isn't unsympathetic. It's the kindest thing you can do.

But what was the problem? What did Jesus want them to 'repent' of? If you've been following him so far, you may know the answer. Ever since that opening sermon in Nazareth, Jesus had been telling people things most of them didn't want to hear. They wanted a rabble-rousing, let's-go-and-bash-the-Romans sort of leader. Jesus went about healing people, talking about a few seeds producing a lot of fruit, and warning the rich and the self-righteous that their cosy world was under judgment. And now we begin to realize what was going on. He could see, more clearly than most of his contemporaries, that Israel was poised on a knife-edge. One false move, one classic piece of anti-Roman activism, and the Romans would come and stamp on the nation once and for all. Jesus is desperate to save his people. He will go ahead and take the full force of Rome's anger onto himself. Anyone who follows him will find that a way of escape. But if they don't – if they embrace the way of violence that he has set his face against – then they are signing their own death warrants. The fruitless tree is asking to be cut down. Stern situations need stern warnings.

Today

All right, you can take your hands off your ears now. Put them together in prayer, and pray that Jesus' warnings about the dangers of violent nationalism may be heard in our world, which still needs those warnings so badly.

WEEK 3: SUNDAY

Psalm 63.1–8

¹O God, you are my God, I seek you, my soul thirsts for you;
  my flesh faints for you, as in a dry and weary land
  where there is no water.
²So I have looked upon you in the sanctuary,
  beholding your power and glory.
³Because your steadfast love is better than life,
  my lips will praise you.
⁴So I will bless you as long as I live;
  I will lift up my hands and call on your name.
⁵My soul is satisfied as with a rich feast,
  and my mouth praises you with joyful lips.
⁶When I think of you on my bed,
  and meditate on you in the watches of the night;
⁷for you have been my help,
  and in the shadow of your wings I sing for joy.
⁸My soul clings to you;
  your right hand upholds me.

So: it's getting tough now.

Whatever your Lenten discipline, by this stage it should be starting to bite. This Psalm will help when that happens.

This Psalm brings us, in heart and mind, into God's Temple, the 'sanctuary' in Jerusalem. That's where the Psalmist remembers 'looking upon God' and 'beholding his power and glory'. Wherever the pilgrim would go afterwards, he or she would carry with them the memory of that time, and the constant reminder of God's majesty.

The Temple in the Old Testament comes into the New Testament wearing skin, bones and flesh. Jesus himself is the true Temple, the place on earth where the living God dwells with his people, revealing his power and glory. That is the message of the whole New Testament, particularly John's gospel and certain passages in Paul. So when we read psalms like this we should get used to 'translating' them: references to the Temple are drawn towards Jesus, and references to the 'sanctuary' spring into new life when we think of the Word made Flesh, the personal presence of the living God. When we worship Jesus – when we come into the presence of his power and glory in word and sacrament, in prayer and in ministry to the poor – that gaze is meant to sustain us in all the dry and dusty places we then have to experience.

But there is a second sense in which the Temple becomes human in the New Testament. By the Holy Spirit, we ourselves, who follow Jesus and recognize him as the human face of the living God, are called to be 'a holy Temple in the Lord', 'a dwelling place of God in the Spirit' (Ephesians 2.21–22). When we meet together as Christians and when, throughout the day and week, we are consciously living as part of the family of Jesus' people, we are not simply offering mutual encouragement and support in the practice of our faith. We are being God's Temple, the place that God fills with his presence in advance of the time when he will fill the whole world with his love and renewing, healing power (Ephesians 1.23).

These are the realities we need to go back to, in mind and heart, when things are difficult, like the pilgrim going through dry and dusty valleys.

Today

'Because your steadfast love is better than life, my lips will praise you.'

'For you have been my help, and in the shadow of your wings I sing for joy.'

Make these promises, these realities, your meditation, by day and in the small hours of the night (verse 6).

Cling on to them until you realize that, actually, it's *God's* right hand that is holding on to *you*.

WEEK 3: MONDAY

Luke 9.37–62; focused on 9.57–62

[57]As they were going along the road a man addressed Jesus.

'Wherever you're going,' he said, 'I'll follow you!'

[58]'Foxes have lairs,' Jesus replied, 'and the birds of the sky have nests; but the son of man doesn't have anywhere to lay his head.'

[59]To another person he said, 'Follow me.' But he replied,

'Master, let me first go and bury my father.'

[60]'Let the dead bury their dead,' said Jesus. 'You must go and announce God's kingdom.'

[61]'I will follow you, Master,' said another, 'but first let me say goodbye to the people at home.'

[62]'Nobody,' replied Jesus, 'who begins to plough and then looks over his shoulder is fit for God's kingdom.'

So: what's your excuse?

One of my students once gave me, as a present, a book called something like *The Penguin Book of Excuses*. It was supposed to remind me of all the times when he'd turned up late, or not handed an essay in on time, and had come up with more and more wonderful 'reasons' for why things hadn't worked out.

Sooner or later, most of us who know in our heart of hearts we want to follow Jesus find ourselves coming up with excuses as to why his particularly sharp demands don't really apply to us.

God knows we're human and need a rhythm of rest and refreshment. But God also knows, and Jesus obviously knew, that once we start down that road it's easy to make exceptions to all the rules when it comes to our own case. So the demand goes out. Now in this way, now in that way, Jesus is saying, 'Look! This is God's kingdom we're talking about, not a comfortable way of being religious that will let you settle down and take life at your own pace!' Are you up for that?

Yes, I know: those were special circumstances. Jesus' public career was short, and he needed people to get on with the job at once. And yes, many of us are called to get into a longer-term mode, not to burn out with frenetic activity in a short sprint. But, again, you can't use that as an excuse for avoiding the sharp edges of God's call. Jesus never said, 'Come with me and all your happiest dreams will be fulfilled.' He said, 'Take up your cross and follow me.' Don't expect an easy time; having nowhere to call 'home' may come with the job. Don't expect that you will be able to fulfil all your social obligations: 'burying your father', whether literally or metaphorically, was one of the highest obligations in Jewish society, and Jesus says that the demands of the kingdom come before it.

And, finally, plough a straight furrow. Looking back to see whether it's been straight so far will guarantee that the next bit won't be.

Today

Talk to God about the excuses you make to him. Ask him to help you to follow him wherever he leads, and to give you the strength not to look back.

WEEK 3: TUESDAY

Luke 10; focused on 10.25–37

[25]A lawyer got up and put Jesus on the spot.

'Teacher,' he said, 'what should I do to inherit the life of the coming age?'

[26]'Well,' replied Jesus, 'what is written in the law? What's your interpretation of it?'

[27]'You shall love the Lord your God', he replied, 'with all your heart, all your soul, all your strength, and all your understanding; and your neighbour as yourself.'

[28]'Well said!' replied Jesus. 'Do that and you will live.'

²⁹'Ah,' said the lawyer, wanting to win the point, 'but who is my neighbour?'

³⁰Jesus rose to the challenge. 'Once upon a time,' he said, 'a man was going down from Jerusalem to Jericho, and was set upon by brigands. They stripped him and beat him and ran off leaving him half dead. ³¹A priest happened to be going down that road, and when he saw him he went past on the opposite side. ³²So too a Levite came by the place; he saw him too, and went past on the opposite side.

³³'But a travelling Samaritan came to where he was. When he saw him he was filled with pity. ³⁴He came over to him and bound up his wounds, pouring in oil and wine. Then he put him on his own beast, took him to an inn, and looked after him. ³⁵The next morning, as he was going on his way, he gave the innkeeper two day's wages. "Take care of him," he said, "and on my way back I'll pay you whatever else you need to spend on him."

³⁶'Which of these three do you think turned out to be the neighbour of the man who was set upon by the brigands?'

³⁷'The one who showed mercy on him,' came the reply.

'Well,' Jesus said to him, 'you go and do the same.'

The danger is that we think we know this story by heart. Today, read it slowly, again and again, and allow yourself to stand by the side of the road and watch what's happening.

Or imagine *you* were the one going down from Jerusalem to Jericho... The moment of fear as you go round that corner by the big rock, a long way away from towns or cities; the moment of panic as they come at you, the sharp, sickening pain as they beat you up; then the sense of being too weak either to resist or to pick yourself up from the ditch where they've left you...

Then, with your whole body screaming for help but without the breath to cry out, a moment of hope... Footsteps, coming up the hill. Please, please help! They're coming closer... surely they must have seen me... and then they go on by, fainter and fainter, dying away. Despair.

Then it happens again! More footsteps. Surely this time they'll help me. But they don't.

Then another. This time there's a donkey as well. You hear it snuffling. Then a voice. A strange accent. A flowing of oil and wine into sharp, stinging wounds. Strong, gentle arms. The warmth of the donkey's back. Every step a wrench of pain, but at least you're going somewhere. Then, as you drift in and out of consciousness, voices. The chink of a coin. A bed. A sigh of relief.

At one level (and this is a level many great Christian teachers have exploited) that's what the story is about: you and me, wounded by sin, the world and the devil, and left for dead by the road; and Jesus as the stranger who comes to rescue us. Yes, that's fine as far as it goes. But there is more.

Because the rescuer is one of those dreadful Samaritans. In Jesus' day, that meant (to a Jew), 'the other lot', 'those people up there who hate us and whom we hate back'. Keep well away, says the world. We are different.

So, all of a sudden, I have to think again about who God's kingdom is really for. Is Jesus saying that God's kingdom has all sorts of people in it I never expected? That, certainly, is what the first Christians discovered very soon.

The question, now as then, is whether we will use all that Jesus is telling us here about love and grace as a call to extend that love and grace to the whole world. No church, no Christian can remain content with living life in a way that allows us to watch most of the world lying half-dead in the road and pass by.

Today

Ask Jesus to help you to see the people you are passing by on the other side.

WEEK 3: WEDNESDAY

Luke 11.1–28; focused on 11.1–8

[1]Once Jesus was praying in a particular place. When he had finished, one of his disciples approached.

'Teach us to pray, Master,' he said, 'just like John taught his disciples.'

[2]'When you pray,' replied Jesus, 'this is what to say:

'Father, may your name be honoured; may your kingdom come; [3]give us each day our daily bread; [4]and forgive us our sins, since we too forgive all our debtors; and don't put us to the test.

[5]'Suppose one of you has a friend,' he said, 'and you go to him in the middle of the night and say, "My dear friend, lend me three loaves of bread! [6]A friend of mine is on a journey and has arrived at my house, and I have nothing to put in front of him!" [7]He will answer from inside his house, "Don't make life difficult for me! The door is already shut, and my children and I are all in bed! I can't get up and give you anything." [8]Let me tell you, even if he won't get up and give you anything just because you're his friend, because of your shameless persistence he will get up and give you whatever you need.'

'How long do I have to go on praying about it?' I asked my spiritual director. I was faced with a peculiarly intractable problem and there seemed no obvious way out. I had prayed about it already for quite some time and there seemed to be no change.

'You can never tell,' he replied with a gentle smile. 'Perhaps every day for a month or two. Or it might be a year or two. The timing isn't our business; that's up to God. Our task is to go on praying and trust that God will do what he will do in his own time.'

That was really frustrating advice, but it turned out to be right. It was two or three more months before anything happened, but when it did it was like a dam bursting. I have no idea why God answers on the 1000th time a prayer he seems to have ignored for the previous 999 times. One might imagine that it would work more steadily and gradually. But no: from our point of view at least, prayer is like chopping at a tree. For 99 strokes of the axe, the main trunk seems to stand firm. Then, on the 100th stroke, suddenly it keels over.

Of course, we know that the previous strokes of the axe were weakening the trunk, even though we couldn't see it. And that's what prayer is like – not that God needs 'weakening' but that, for all sorts of other reasons that we can't see, things have to take the time they have to take. And that leads us to the shape of the prayer Jesus gave his disciples. However you pray it, the Lord's Prayer starts precisely with the note that says, 'God's way and God's time is best.'

To say the Lord's Prayer demands that you pay primary attention to God himself. It is *his* name and *his* kingdom that we care about above all, not our particular problems. But, having said that, the three requests that follow – for bread, forgiveness, and safety from being tested to destruction – all place our concerns *within* that name and kingdom. That's the clue.

To pray the Lord's Prayer, then, requires an odd combination: complete humility and complete boldness. Once we get the first right, the second can follow cheerfully. Once God's name and kingdom are the framework of all we do and think, we are free to knock on his door as late at night as we want.

Today

Try to find some occasions to pray the Lord's Prayer very slowly, as if you were praying it for the first time. Think particularly about the words, 'Hallowed be thy name; thy kingdom come, thy will be done.' Imagine what it will be like when God's kingdom is here on earth as it is in heaven. Does that help you to see Jesus' prayer in a new way?

WEEK 3: THURSDAY
Luke 11.29–53; focused on 11.33–36

[33]'Nobody lights a lamp in order to hide it or put it under a jug. They put it on a lampstand, so that people who come in can see the light.
[34]'Your eye is the lamp of your body. If your eye is focused, your whole body is full of light. But if it's evil, your body is in darkness. [35]Watch out, then, in case the light inside you turns to darkness. [36]If your whole body is illuminated, with no part in darkness, everything will be illuminated, just as you are by a flash of lightning.'

Here is an exercise for the middle of Lent. Note down, every hour or at least three times a day, the main things you have looked at, gazed at, allowed your eyes to rest on during the day.

Quite telling, isn't it? For some of us, alas, a computer screen would be high on the list – but the question would then be, 'What's on the screen?' What images and messages are getting beamed into your whole body, your whole person, by the searchlight that Jesus is talking about?

Listening to what Jesus says here, we may find it puzzling. We think of a lamp as something that shines outwards – like a miner wearing a hat with a torch on it so he can see underground. But Jesus seems to be using the picture the other way round. The inner depths of the personality (the word 'body' here really means 'the whole person') are in darkness, and need to be illuminated. And, Jesus is saying, the thing that will illuminate them is the thing on which you fasten your gaze.

So take the test a stage further. When you think about the things you've gazed at today, or in the last few days, how have they affected the person you are? Have you allowed your eye to rest on, and feast on, genuine beauty? The eye is one of our principal means of finding our way within God's beautiful creation; are you allowing your eyes to draw in the light of that beauty to make your whole personality beautiful as a result?

Have you allowed your eye to rest on, to concern itself with, the injustices of the world, the places where people cry out to God for hope and help because they are being trampled underfoot by careless and arrogant people and systems? Or are you allowing yourself to be a mere spectator, looking on as though with a bird's-eye view but without any real engagement with what's happening?

Gazing on the beauty of God's world on the one hand, and on its need for justice on the other, will illuminate the body, the whole person, so that it celebrates the glory of God and works for his kingdom. What would Jesus say if he saw so many of us spending our time, and our sight, on things that are either worthless or actually damaging? How much of our popular entertainment, especially on television, would make Jesus say 'Didn't I tell you not to put a jug over the light? How do you expect your whole person to be illuminated if you don't let genuine light come through your eyes into your innermost being?'

Lent leads us to the foot of the cross. Two millennia of Christians have found gazing at the cross of Jesus, however it is depicted, to be both one of the most beautiful sights they can imagine and one of the most impassioned pleas for justice. In 2000 the National Gallery in London put on an exhibition called 'Seeing Salvation', consisting mostly of images of the crucifixion. The newspapers scoffed. But the public came in their tens of thousands, and gazed and gazed.

Today

What have you gazed on in the last couple of days? What would you like to gaze on today?

WEEK 3: FRIDAY

Luke 12.1–34; focused on 12.22–32

[22]'So let me tell you this,' he said to the disciples. 'Don't be anxious about your life – what you should eat; or about your body – what you should wear. [23]Life is more than food! The body is more than clothing! [24]Think about the ravens: they don't sow seed, they don't gather harvests, they don't have storehouses or barns; and God feeds them. How much more will he feed you! Think of the difference between yourselves and the birds!

[25]'Which of you by being anxious can add a day to your lifetime? [26]So if you can't even do a little thing like that, why worry about anything else? [27]Think about the lilies and the way they grow. They don't work hard, they don't weave cloth; but, let me tell you, not even Solomon in all his glory was dressed up like one of them. [28]So if that's how God clothes the grass in the field – here today, into the fire tomorrow – how much more will he clothe you, you little-faith lot!

[29]'So don't you go hunting about for what to eat or what to drink, and don't be anxious. [30]The nations of the world go searching for all that stuff, and your Father knows you need it. [31]This is what you should search for: God's kingdom! Then all the rest will be given you as well. [32]Don't be afraid, little flock. Your Father is delighted to give you the kingdom.'

Jesus relished the goodness and beauty of the natural world, and so should we.

It's strange, considering just how much beauty is all around us, that the modern world has trained itself to ignore it for much of the time. But not only is it a delight to the eyes and the mind; it is a great school of prayer.

Stand beside a field full of wheat, or barley, or some other great crop. Watch the sun bringing out the colour. Watch the wind rippling through and making patterns, and the grain, supple but strong, springing back into shape. Then think of the way we humans are meant to flourish, with the love of God looking down on us and the fresh wind of the Spirit bringing out patterns and meanings in our lives – corporate as well as individual. Reflect on the strange interconnectedness of it all. And, in thanking God for the mystery of our life, learn to trust him in new ways and at new levels.

Or get the binoculars out and watch the birds – yes, the ravens if you've got some handy, but whatever birds there are available. Get to know the way they organize their lives – or, it seems sometimes, disorganize them; and yet the way in which they flourish. Watch, for instance, the way in which a flock of a hundred or more seabirds will fly in exact formation, at high speed, and then, more dramatic than a squadron of display aircraft, all turn at precisely the same moment.

Reflect on the ways in which God has so implanted a sense of how to be, how to live, how to play even, within these tiny creatures which, Jesus assures us, are not nearly as highly valued as ourselves. And learn, in prayer, the art of recognizing that God the creator has formed us to live and move and have our being within his world, and of trusting him in everything.

Learn, in other words, the gentle but powerful secrets of God's kingdom. Much of today's world seems hell-bent on stopping us learning that lesson, on teaching us an 'independence' that turns out to be nothing more than the sulk of a rebellious teenager. Strange as it may seem – though not to those who practise prayer within the rhythms and beauties of God's creation – we are most truly ourselves when we are most truly living under the sovereign rule of God. 'Search for God's kingdom!' Ask God in prayer how you can be part of that great purpose of new creation. He will be only too pleased to show you.

Today

Try to spend some time looking at something around you more slowly and with greater attention than you normally do.

Is there something you don't normally notice that makes you want to give thanks to God?

WEEK 3: SATURDAY
Luke 15.1–3, 11b–32

[1]All the tax-collectors and sinners were coming close to listen to Jesus. [2]The Pharisees and the legal experts were grumbling. 'This fellow welcomes sinners!' they said. 'He even eats with them!'

[3]So Jesus told them this parable… [11b]'Once there was a man who had two sons. [12]The younger son said to the father, "Father, give me my share in the property." So he divided up his livelihood between them. [13]Not many days later the younger son turned his share into cash, and set off for a country far away, where he spent his share in having a riotous good time.

[15]'When he had spent it all, a severe famine came on that country, and he found himself destitute. [15]So he went and attached himself to one of the citizens of that country, who sent him into the fields to feed his pigs. [16]He longed to satisfy his hunger with the pods that the pigs were eating, and nobody gave him anything.

[17]'He came to his senses. "Just think!" he said to himself. "There are all my father's hired hands with plenty to eat – and here am I, starving to death! [18]I shall get up and go to my father, and I'll say to him: 'Father; I have sinned against heaven and before you; [19]I don't deserve to be called your son any longer. Make me like one of your hired hands.'" [20]And he got up and went to his father.

'While he was still a long way off, his father saw him and his heart was stirred with love and pity. He ran to him, hugged him tight, and kissed him. [21]"Father," the son began, "I have sinned against heaven and before you; I don't deserve to be called your son any longer." [22]But the father said to his servants, "Hurry! Bring the best clothes and put them on him! Put a ring on his hand, and shoes on his feet! [23]And bring the calf that we've fattened up, kill it, and let's eat and have a party! [24]This son of mine was dead, and is alive again! He was lost, and now he's found!" And they began to celebrate.

²⁵'The older son was out in the fields. When he came home, and got near to the house, he heard music and dancing. ²⁶He called one of the servants and asked what was going on.

²⁷'"Your brother's come home!" he said. "And your father has thrown a great party – he's killed the fattened calf! – because he's got him back safe and well!"

²⁸'He flew into a rage, and wouldn't go in.

'Then his father came out and pleaded with him. ²⁹"Look here!" he said to his father, "I've been slaving for you all these years! I've never disobeyed a single commandment of yours. And you never even gave me a young goat so I could have a party with my friends. ³⁰But when this son of yours comes home, once he's finished gobbling up your livelihood with his whores, you kill the fattened calf for him!"

³¹'"My son," he replied, "you're always with me. Everything I have belongs to you. ³²But we had to celebrate and be happy! This brother of yours was dead and is alive again! He was lost, and now he's found!"'

'We just *had* to have a party!'

That's the main point of this story. Jesus had been challenged about the parties he was having, and the company he was keeping at them, and he responded with this spectacular story. Let's go to one of those parties and see what it was all about.

We sneak in at the back and find things already in full flow. A bit of a rough crowd, it seems – the sort of people you'd probably avoid in the street, some of them scruffy, some of them a bit too suspiciously well dressed. (How could they afford clothes like *that*?) Somebody's obviously been hard at work cooking, because there are delicious smells coming from a back room and people keep emerging from the kitchen with more dishes. And there are flagons of wine and everyone is helping themselves... and in the middle of it all we spot Jesus himself, relaxed and easy, reclining as people did on a couch beside the table, chatting to the man beside him, occasionally flashing a smile at the serving-girls bringing more food, or waving to a newcomer who's heard there's a party and has pushed his way in. Occasionally we hear snatches of what Jesus is saying. Something about the first being last and the last first. The man he's talking to looks surprised; he wants to believe it but isn't yet sure he can.

But at the back of the crowd, where we're standing, there are other voices. *What on earth is he up to now?* Isn't he supposed to be a prophet? Isn't he telling people about God's kingdom? Doesn't that mean being holy, not messing around with the rabble? And if he's teaching people to call God 'Father', doesn't he know that sons are supposed to obey their Father's commandments? He's just a glutton and a drunkard like them – and the Bible warned us about teachers like that!

Eventually Jesus looks up, and glances round the room towards the whisperers. The talking dies down as people wait to see what he's going to say. All right, you want to know why there's a party? You want to know how it is with fathers and sons? And out it comes: a masterpiece, one of the greatest stories ever told, echoing the ancient stories of those other ill-starred brothers, Cain and Abel, Ishmael and Isaac, and particularly Esau and Jacob. The son who runs away in trouble and comes back to find resentment. But all with a new twist. *Something new is going on, right here, right now, and a party is the only possible response.* 'Resurrection' is happening right under your noses, and you can't see it. 'This my son – this your brother – was dead and is alive again. He was lost and is found.'

Today

Imagine you are at a party like the one here. It's happening in the local pub. One of the regulars has just had a very good win on the horses. He's invited all his friends, and all the other regulars, for a really good evening.

There is Jesus, right in the middle of it all. He turns and looks at you, standing by the door. 'Yes,' his eyes seem to say, 'and what about you? Come on in and join the fun.'

Talk to God about how that makes you feel, and what it makes you think.

WEEK 4: SUNDAY

Psalm 32

[1]Happy are those whose transgression is forgiven,
    whose sin is covered.
[2]Happy are those to whom the Lord imputes no iniquity,
    and in whose spirit there is no deceit.
[3]While I kept silence, my body wasted away
    through my groaning all day long.
[4]For day and night your hand was heavy upon me;
    my strength was dried up as by the heat of summer.
[5]Then I acknowledged my sin to you,
    and I did not hide my iniquity;
    I said, 'I will confess my transgressions to the Lord',
    and you forgave the guilt of my sin.
[6]Therefore let all who are faithful offer prayer to you;
    at a time of distress, the rush of mighty waters
    shall not reach them.
[7]You are a hiding place for me; you preserve me
    from trouble;
    you surround me with glad cries of deliverance.
[8]I will instruct you and teach you the way you should go;
    I will counsel you with my eye upon you.
[9]Do not be like a horse or a mule without understanding,
    whose temper must be curbed with bit and bridle,
    else it will not stay near you.
[10]Many are the torments of the wicked,
    but steadfast love surrounds those who trust in the Lord.
[11]Be glad in the Lord and rejoice, O righteous,
    and shout for joy, all you upright in heart.

Forgiveness is, simply, the most powerful thing in the world.

Most people never realize that, more's the pity. In fact, there are many cultures in which forgiveness is seen as a sign of weakness, and 'compassion' is regarded as just being wet and wishy-washy. Many individuals live their whole lives by that rule. They don't want to offer forgiveness and compassion to other people, and they certainly don't want to admit that they need it themselves.

But when you've been forgiven, your life will change in a way that nothing else will achieve. A sense of freedom, of a new start, of fresh possibilities, of the dark and gloomy clouds rolling away and the sun coming out and bathing the whole landscape with glorious, pure light. It's as though you've been trying to listen to some great music, but the electrical system is messed up and the speakers aren't working properly, and the whole thing is crackling and popping – and then, suddenly, somebody fixes it, and the room is filled with a glorious sound. You'd forgotten it could be like that.

Lent is a great time to do the spring cleaning, to go looking into the dark corners of the heart and mind and life, to see where the dust has been getting in, where spiders have left cobwebs, where items that should have been washed and cleaned and put away properly are lying around under the furniture. You may need some help with this, and that's what clergy, spiritual directors and other pastors are there for. But, in particular, you need the encouragement of scriptures like Psalm 32, reminding you that it's worthwhile, that whatever grubby corners you come across can be cleaned up and made into places of beauty. Refusing to confess sin really does cramp your style, spiritually, psychologically and perhaps physically too (verses 3–4).

But there's more. Once the room is swept and clean, we find it might be time to rearrange the furniture and use the room for new purposes. When God forgives, he does so not in order to bring us back from being 'in the red' merely to having a 'zero' balance. He does so in order to guide us into new tasks and callings he's had in mind all along, but for which we weren't ready.

Lent is about that, too, and the two things – forgiveness and a new calling – belong closely together. All work for God's kingdom, not only the well-known 'ministries' of the church but all kinds of vocations, flow directly from the forgiving and healing love of God. Without that, we would just be arrogant, imagining that we can sign up to work for God's kingdom in our own power and goodness. But, likewise, all forgiveness flows directly into serving God, his people and his world.

George Herbert, as so often, put it with simple elegance:

'And know you not,' says Love, 'Who bore the blame?'
  'My dear, then I will serve.'
'You must sit down,' says Love, 'and taste my meat.'
  So I did sit and eat.

('Love bade me welcome')

Today

So often we think of 'confessing' as a rather dreary, embarrassing thing, forgetting what a joy it is to know we are 'ransomed, healed, restored, forgiven'.

Is there something that you really need to put behind you, this Lent, once and for all?

WEEK 4: MONDAY

Luke 12.35–59; focused on 12.35–40

[35]'Make sure you're dressed and ready with your lamps alight,' said Jesus. [36]'You need to be like people waiting for their master when he comes back from the wedding-feast, so that when he comes and knocks they will be able to open the door for him at once.' [37]A blessing on the servants whom the master finds awake

when he comes! I'm telling you the truth: he will put on an apron and sit them down and come and wait on them. [38]A blessing on them if he comes in the second watch of the night, or even the third, and finds them like that!

[39]'But you should know this: if the householder had known what time the thief was coming, he wouldn't have let his house be broken into. [40]You too should be ready, because the son of man is coming at a time you don't expect.'

Jesus' teaching about not worrying is balanced here by his warning that we should be alert. ('Be alert,' says the bumper-sticker; 'We need more Lerts.') To rub the point in, he invites us to imagine ourselves going to bed at night but expecting all the time that there might be a burglar on the way.

Today we have complicated locks, bolts and burglar-alarms. In those days you never knew when someone might use the long nights and the unlit streets as an opportunity for a quick intrusion. So you go to sleep with one ear ready, like a sleeping mother still listening out for the cry of her newborn child, for the tell-tale noise of someone forcing the door.

Jesus was getting Israel, and the world, and his followers, ready for great events that were still to come. Everything he was doing was about launching a project, the work of God's kingdom. One day that kingdom will come to birth full and fresh, and all that Jesus has been doing will be seen as the necessary ground-work for that new moment.

But...as with the burglar, nobody knows when it's going to arrive! So the characteristic Christian poise is to be alert, to be ready, like servants waiting for the master of the house to come back from a late-night party.

There are two different dimensions to this challenge.

First, let's imagine ourselves as part of the gaggle of Jesus' followers, moving around Galilee with him and wondering where it's all going to end. Here we are, watching him heal people, sneaking into parties where he's hanging out with people who desperately need his help, hearing him teach about God's coming kingdom when the powerful and arrogant will be overthrown and the weak and poor will be raised up. And, as we try to pray the prayer he's given us, we wonder when it's all going to happen. 'Your kingdom come...'? Wish it would hurry up.

'No,' says Jesus, 'you need to learn to wait. That's part of the point. You need to grow up in your trust of God. Learning to wait is part of the deal.' 'Lord,' we say, 'give us strength and patience – but please hurry up anyway!' 'No,' he says again, 'you've got to be like servants prepared to wait through until the small hours. What matters is that when God does what God is going to do, you're ready.'

And then, one day, it happens: Jesus is arrested, tried, executed; and we're in a panic. The burglar has come and we were asleep... But then, three days later, Jesus is alive again, and he's the true king, and a whole new world has begun.

Ever since that day, the church has spoken the same message: God's kingdom was well and truly launched at the resurrection, but it will be completed when God makes new heavens and new earth, with Jesus present as King and Lord in the middle of it all. We have no idea when that will happen. We have to be ready at any time.

Today

Lord, give us patience, and the courage to wait and watch and be ready for the day when your kingdom comes on earth as in heaven.

WEEK 4: TUESDAY
Luke 13; focused on 13.22–30

²²Jesus went through the towns and villages, teaching as he went, making his way towards Jerusalem.

> [23]'Master,' somebody said to him, 'will there be only a few that are saved?'
>
> [24]'Struggle hard', Jesus replied, 'to get in by the narrow gate. Let me tell you: many will try to get in and won't be able to. [25]When the householder gets up and shuts the door – at that moment you will begin to stand outside and knock at the door and say, "Master, open the door for us." Then he will say in response, "I don't know where you've come from." [26]Then you will begin to say, "We ate with you and drank with you, and you taught in our streets!" [27]And he will say to you, "I don't know where you people are from. Be off with you, you wicked lot."
>
> [28]'That's where you'll find weeping and gnashing of teeth: when you see Abraham and Isaac and Jacob and all the prophets in God's kingdom, and you yourselves thrown out. [29]People will come from east and west, from north and south, and sit down to feast in God's kingdom. [30]And, listen to this: some who are last will be first, and some of the first will be last.'

True prayer is always humble. By definition. True prayer means recognizing that God is God and that we ... aren't. It also means doing something inexplicable in terms of the present world of space, time and matter: it already says, 'I believe in someone who is there, who is my Lord, even though I can't see him.'

So learning to pray means learning to abandon pride. It's easy for those of us who have been brought up as Christians, churchgoers, in a supposedly 'Christian' country, to imagine that we are, as it were, Jesus' natural followers; that we can coast along and get there all right whatever happens. These stern warnings should send us back to our prayers, back to our knees, back to humility and trust. We cannot presume. We dare not.

Jesus had to make exactly that point to his contemporaries. Like John the Baptist before him, he had to warn them that they couldn't assume that being children of Abraham meant they had an inside track, 'a backdoor to heaven' as one of today's Jewish teachers has put it.

Jesus doesn't tell them, in this passage, what they must positively do. He merely warns them against presumption, and tells them that there will come a time when the people who thought they were 'automatically' part of God's people will find they're outside, while plenty who never imagined they'd have anything to do with the family of Abraham, Isaac and Jacob will be inside.

The shocking warning to the insiders is matched by the surprising grace towards the outsiders. That fits exactly with the constant theme we've found, for instance in the Beatitudes and Woes: blessings on all the wrong people, woes on all the right ones! That puts the pressure on those of us who might assume that we are the 'right' ones: to recognize, both in how we pray and what we pray, that everything we have, everything we are, is a gift from God, and that neither we nor anybody else deserve it.

Prayer like that will be humble. It will also be a sigh of relief. We don't have anything to prove, anything to earn.

Today

Thank you, Father, for your generous love. Help me, today and every day, to trust in you, not in myself.

WEEK 4: WEDNESDAY
Luke 14; focused on 14.25–33

[25]A large crowd was gathering around him. Jesus turned to face them.

[26]'If any of you come to me,' he said to them, 'and don't hate your father and your mother, your wife and your children, your brothers and your sisters – yes, and even your own life! – you can't be my disciple. [27]If you don't pick up your own cross and come after me, you can't be my disciple.

[28]'Don't you see? Supposing one of you wants to build a tower; what will you do? You will first of all sit down and work out how

much it will cost, to see whether you have enough to finish it.
²⁹Otherwise, when you've laid the foundation and then can't
finish it, everyone who sees it will begin to make fun of you.
³⁰"Here's a fellow", they'll say, "who began to build but couldn't
finish!"

³¹"Or think of a king, on the way to fight a war against another king. What will he do? He will first sit down and discuss
with his advisors whether, with ten thousand troops, he is going
to be a match for the other side who are coming with twenty
thousand! ³²If they decide he isn't, he will send a delegation,
while the other one is still a long way away, and sue for peace.

³³"In the same way, none of you can be my disciple unless you
give up all your possessions.'

This is another time when you want to put your hands over
your ears, as Jesus says some of the harshest things you've heard
from him yet. Really, you think, if this was all he said, nobody
would ever follow him! Hating your family, giving up your
possessions, carrying your own instrument of torture – what
on earth is he on about? Most Christians in today's world, and
I suspect a good many of Jesus' own hearers, try to avoid or
ignore this kind of stuff.

That would be a mistake, albeit a natural one. Let's think
about what Jesus was up against.

He was announcing God's new way of running things. He
was telling God's people that everything up to now had been
preparation, but he was starting the real thing. And the hardest
task for someone doing that is to persuade people to give up
the preparatory stages they've become so comfortable with.

What were those preparatory stages? For Jesus' people,
ancient Israel, there were two stages in particular: family and
land. Israel was identified as Abraham's family, a single ethnic
unit. (True, some people came in from outside, like Ruth in the
Old Testament; but they were still basically a people defined by
family identity.) And they were also identified as the people

who lived in a special land: that beautiful but highly contested small country in the Middle East. Again, by the time of Jesus more Jews lived away from the land than in it, but they all knew that was their real home. That was their ancestral possession, and woe betide anyone who compromised with it.

Family and possessions: the two things Jesus now says you have to give up. God's people are being redefined, and these identity markers won't matter any more. Cling onto them, and you'll be like people keeping the curtains closed when the sun has risen. That was night-time; this is daytime.

Jesus' challenge, then, comes to all of us at the point where we are tempted to settle down and be comfortable with the way things are. 'No,' he says, 'that would be like someone wanting to build a tower, or fight a battle, without thinking out what's involved.' You need to think through, to pray through, what it's going to mean to be a follower, a learner, a disciple. You don't want to be left high and dry when God's kingdom goes forward and you turn out to have settled for something less.

Today

Ignatius Loyola, the founder of the Jesuit order, used to pray this prayer:

Lord, teach me to be generous,
Teach me to serve you as you deserve:
To give and not to count the cost,
To fight and not to heed the wounds,
To toil and not to seek for rest,
To labour and to ask for no reward,
Save that of knowing that I do your will.

Do you find that an easy prayer to pray?

Talk to God about how that prayer makes you feel and what it makes you think.

WEEK 4: THURSDAY
Luke 15; focused on 15.4–10

[4]"Supposing one of you has a hundred sheep,' he said, 'and you lose one of them. What will you do? Why, you'll leave the ninety-nine out in the countryside, and you'll go off looking for the lost one until you find it! [5]And when you find it, you'll be so happy – you'll put it on your shoulders [6]and come home, and you'll call your friends and neighbours in. "Come and have a party!" you'll say. "Celebrate with me! I've found my lost sheep!"

[7]'Well, let me tell you: that's how glad they will be in heaven over one sinner who repents – more than over ninety-nine righteous people who don't need repentance.

[8]'Or supposing a woman has ten coins and loses one of them. What will she do? Why, she'll light a lamp, and sweep the house, and hunt carefully until she finds it! [9]And when she finds it she'll call her friends and neighbours in. "Come and have a party!" she'll say. "Celebrate with me! I've found my lost coin!"

[10]'Well, let me tell you: that's how glad the angels of God feel when a single sinner repents.'

So: what was it about the sheep that was so special?

Was it the shepherd's favourite? Was it a young lamb he'd always treated like a pet? Did it have a particular bleat that he could always pick out when he listened to the flock, and would always make him smile when he heard it?

Did it have a particularly fine woolly fleece, which he knew would fetch a good price at the next shearing?

No. None of those.

There was only one thing about the lost sheep that drove the shepherd to go looking for it. And that was simply the fact that it was lost. Nothing more, nothing less.

All right, it's only a story: part of the set of Jesus' this-is-why-we're-having-a-party stories. But, like most of Jesus' stories, this one connects with what goes on in people's heads when they respond to him. So many of us secretly assume that there must be something special about this person, or that one, that makes Jesus go looking for them. Some people, brimful of self-confidence, always assume that they are one of the special ones. (Someone gave a friend of mine a T-shirt that read 'Jesus loves you, but I'm his favourite'.) Others, with low self-esteem, always assume that it's the other people who are the special ones, and that they're somewhere in the back of the flock, unnoticed and unimportant.

But the point is that every single sheep is important to the shepherd, and when any one of them gets into difficulties he is especially concerned for them. That is the truth that's so hard to learn, both for those with self-confidence and for those without it.

This story not only connects with the personal thoughts and feelings of those who hear it, but also with passages in the Old Testament, where the picture of a shepherd searching for straying sheep is an image of the coming Messiah and even of God himself. That's why there's a party: God is looking for lost sheep, and when he finds them the angels sing for joy.

As they do, also, for the lost coin. This is a particularly powerful image for a woman, especially in Jesus' culture. The ten coins may well have been part of a special set, perhaps her dowry. (There is some evidence of brides wearing a special headdress that included such coins.) Anyway, once more it's a good reason to celebrate, to have a party.

There's a sting in the tail of these little stories, in case anyone should think (as some people do today) that the whole point is simply Jesus' desire to 'include' anybody and everybody. 'There is joy', he says, 'among the angels in heaven *when a sinner repents*.' Just as the 'Prodigal Son' doesn't stroll home, whistling a cheerful tune, confident that his soft-hearted old father will take him back in, so the people with whom Jesus was celebrating were showing that they wanted their lives to change. By welcoming Jesus, they were inviting him to do in their moral and spiritual lives what he did for so many people physically. Jesus welcomed sinners; but by the time he'd finished with them, they weren't sinners any more.

Today

Lord, help us to celebrate your welcoming love, and be transformed by it.

WEEK 4: FRIDAY
Luke 16; focused on 16.1–12

[1]Jesus said to his disciples, 'Once there was a rich man who had a steward, and charges were laid against him that he was squandering his property. [2]So he called him and said to him, "What's all this I hear about you? Present an account of your stewardship; I'm not going to have you as my steward any more!"

[3]'At this, the steward said to himself, "What shall I do? My master is taking away my stewardship from me! I can't do manual work, and I'd be ashamed to beg...

[4]"I have an idea what to do! – so that people will welcome me into their households when I am fired from being steward."

[5]'So he called his master's debtors to him, one by one. "How much", he asked the first, "do you owe my master?"

[6]"A hundred measures of olive oil," he replied.

'"Take your bill," he said to him, "sit down quickly, and make it fifty."

[7]'To another he said, "And how much do you owe?"

'"A hundred measures of wheat," he replied.

'"Take your bill," he said, "and make it eighty."

[8]'And the master praised the dishonest steward because he had acted wisely. The children of this world, you see, are wiser than the children of light when it comes to dealing with their own generation.

[9]'So let me tell you this: use that dishonest stuff called money to make yourselves friends! Then, when it gives out, they will welcome you into homes that will last.

> [10]'Someone who is faithful in a small matter', Jesus continued, 'will also be faithful in a large one. Someone who is dishonest in a small matter will also be dishonest in a large one. [11]If you haven't been faithful with that wicked thing called money, who is going to entrust you with true wealth? [12]And if you haven't been faithful in looking after what belongs to someone else, who is going to give you what is your own?'

This parable carries a health warning: 'Do Not Try This At Home.' Remember, it is after all a *parable*; it isn't advice on how to run a household.

But what is it a parable *about*?

Jesus' first hearers would have had no problem answering that one. In their world, a story about a landowner and his steward, or manager, was almost certainly a story about God and Israel. And, granted what Jesus had been saying about needing to sit loose to the traditional Jewish attachments to family and land, this would make a whole lot of sense. The nation of Israel, *as a nation*, is going to find that God's purpose is moving ahead in a new direction, as always intended; but if they have been faithless to that overall intention, as Jesus is constantly warning that they have been, then they cannot presume that they will be God's 'steward' for ever and ever.

So what are they to do? 'You must figure out', Jesus is saying, 'how to make friends wherever you can. You're going to need them.' There may be a bit of 'local colour' at this point in the story, because the amounts the steward knocks off the bill for his master's clients may correspond to the amount of interest charged for such loans. Jews weren't supposed to charge interest at all, but many did, and the steward had discovered a way of making friends while putting his master in a position where he couldn't charge him for dishonesty without admitting that he himself had been engaging in illegal practices.

That well illustrates the murky world you get into when you start playing around with money and property. Do one shady deal and others will follow as a way of hushing things up, and before you know what's happened you're in over your head and can't get out. That's the point at which, after the parable, Jesus turns to serious warnings. These are things we need to take very, very seriously. But how?

Jesus has some questions for every generation, for each of his followers. Questions about priorities. Questions about people poorer than you. How are you going to listen to those questions, and answer them truthfully?

Today

Take a walk (in your imagination) to your bank. Take Jesus with you. Chat to him, on the way, about how much money comes in, how big your overdraft is, which loans you hope to pay off, and all that. He will understand; he and Joseph used to be in business, after all. But he still has some questions.

Then, when you get to the bank, sit down in a private room with your manager, with Jesus beside you. Get the full bank statements from last year. Talk through them with Jesus.

Are there points you're tempted to gloss over, or bits you wish had been deleted in advance?

Lord Jesus, make me faithful in little things and great things, so that I may be faithful to your gift to me also.

WEEK 4: SATURDAY

John 12.1–8

[1]Six days before the Passover, Jesus came to Bethany. Lazarus was there, the man he had raised from the dead. [2]So they made a dinner for him there. Martha served, and Lazarus was among the company at table with him.

³Then Mary took a pound of very expensive perfume, made of nard. She anointed Jesus' feet with it, and wiped his feet with her hair. The house was filled with the smell of the perfume.

⁴At this, Judas Iscariot, one of his disciples (the one who was going to betray him), spoke up.

⁵'Why wasn't this ointment sold?' he asked. 'It would have fetched a year's wages! You could have given it to the poor!'

(⁶He didn't say this because he cared for the poor, but because he was a thief. He kept the common purse, and used to help himself to what was in it.)

⁷'Let her alone,' replied Jesus. 'It's all about keeping it for the day of my burial! ⁸You always have the poor with you, but you won't always have me.'

As we approach Passion Sunday, we switch to John's gospel to help us get our hearts and minds ready for the tumultuous, awe-inspiring events that are about to unfold.

John starts by describing a scene that, initially, appears anything but awe-inspiring. It is, rather, very intimate. Mary anoints Jesus' feet with a very expensive perfume, and wipes them with her hair. (There is no reason to suppose that this is another telling of the scene we find in Luke 7, or that the woman in either case was Mary Magdalene; 'Mary' was by far the most common girl's name among first-century Jews.)

Imagine you are Judas, watching the scene. It's been quite a time the last week or two, because Jesus has raised Lazarus from the dead, and there's been a huge fuss about that – some thinking that Jesus can do no wrong and others that he's the most dangerous man on the planet. We're not sure what he's planning next but here we are, nearly in Jerusalem, and everyone's getting excited because it's almost Passover time and if God is ever going to act to free his people then Passover would be the obvious time to do it...

And now, suddenly, this woman seems to be going crazy. Letting her hair loose as if she's trying to seduce someone.

Someone like Jesus! Some mistake, surely. What's she up to? People will talk. Jesus really should have more sense. He ought to realize what people will make of all this. And that smell – perfume that good must have cost a year's wages! Doesn't she know there are poor people around here who could live on that money? Doesn't she realize we're all poor anyway and some of us could use a bit of a bonus after all we've been through... Anyway, Jesus doesn't need his feet washing in that stuff. He must be embarrassed. He probably wants her to stop but is too kind to say so. Maybe one of us had better say something... Maybe it had better be me. I seem to be the only one with any sense just now. Right, then, here goes...

And you suddenly realize, as you live within the character of Judas, that you have got it all very badly wrong. The trouble is, Mary has seen something you hadn't seen, something that the original Judas probably never did see. Learning to see that is what living with Jesus and his story is all about.

Today

Lord, help me to be humble enough to see what you are seeing, even when all my instincts are telling me the opposite. Help me, particularly, to understand what your death was all about.

WEEK 5: SUNDAY

Psalm 126

¹When the Lord restored the fortunes of Zion,
  we were like those who dream.
²Then our mouth was filled with laughter,
  and our tongue with shouts of joy;
  then it was said among the nations, 'The Lord has done great
  things for them.'
³The Lord has done great things for us,
  and we rejoiced.

⁴Restore our fortunes, O Lord,
   like the watercourses in the Negeb.
⁵May those who sow in tears
   reap with shouts of joy.
⁶Those who go out weeping, bearing the seed for sowing,
   shall come home with shouts of joy,
   carrying their sheaves.

Imagine yourself a small child, peacefully at home with your parents and siblings, when suddenly the soldiers come. Rough hands, arrogant voices. 'Everybody out! No time to pack. Line up! Hurry up!' We're out of here. A few men try to resist; swords flash, women scream...Unburied bodies in the village street.

Then the long, dusty journey across the desert. You can still remember, seventy years later, the daytime heat and the chilly nights. At last, you reach a great city where you're treated as curiosities: 'Oh, they finally caught up with you silly Judaeans, did they? Well, you're going to have fun singing your fancy songs here!'

Eventually the little clusters of families find somewhere to live. They do their best to remember, to remember: to tell the stories, to keep the commandments, to forge strong bonds, as you only really do when life's like that. And, yes, to sing the songs, even though they taste bitter in the mouth when you think of Jerusalem in ruins.

You remember now the years that followed: praying, fasting, studying, growing up, marrying, having children, still tasting the bitterness and wondering why you bother going on hoping. Everybody knows that exiles don't return. The dream is over. Better just get used to being in a new place. Forget your old culture: you've got to go on, not back. All peoples think they're special, and then discover that it's just a grandiose fantasy. But still you, and quite a few others, go on praying and re-membering. And singing.

And then...it hardly seems possible, but now at last, in your mid-seventies, it's happened. A new king with a new policy. The Judaeans are to go home! They must rebuild their Temple! This is amazing! The Lord has visited his people!

Now it's time for a new song: 'When the Lord restored the fortunes of Zion, we were like those who dream: laughter in our mouths, songs of joy on our tongues, and everybody looking on and saying "Their God has done great things for them."'

Restoration. Forgiveness. New starts. These are the greatest moments in the world, even if you have to wait a lifetime for them to come.

But then the Psalm turns a corner and looks at projects still unfinished, sorrows still unhealed. 'Do it again, gracious Lord: you brought us back. It was impossible but you did it; now turn things around again for us.' Once again we're sowing in tears, but may we reap with shouts of joy. From exile and return to seedtime and harvest, but it's the same picture.

This is a picture we can make our own as we go through Lent, just as Jesus made it his own as he went through his own Lent, speaking of seeds being strangely and sadly sown so that a great harvest might come up.

Today

Have there been moments in your life when suddenly everything turned round for you or for somebody else? When tears or a long time of difficulty gave way to shouts of joy?

If there have, then today could be a good day to remember them and thank God for them.

WEEK 5: MONDAY

Luke 17; focused on 17.11–19

¹¹As Jesus was on his way to Jerusalem, he passed along the borderlands between Samaria and Galilee. ¹²As he was going into

74

one particular village he was met by ten men with virulent skin diseases who stayed at some distance from him.

¹³'Jesus, Master!' they called out loudly. 'Have pity on us!'

¹⁴When Jesus saw them he said to them, 'Go and show yourselves to the priests.' And as they went, they were healed.

¹⁵One of them, seeing that he had been healed, turned back and gave glory to God at the top of his voice. ¹⁶He fell on his face in front of Jesus' feet and thanked him. He was a Samaritan.

¹⁷'There were ten of you healed, weren't there?' responded Jesus. 'Where are the nine? ¹⁸Is it really the case that the only one who had the decency to give God the glory was this foreigner?

¹⁹'Get up, and be on your way,' he said to him. 'Your faith has saved you.'

When we looked at the parables of the lost sheep and the lost coin, there was one lost in each case while the rest were safe. This time it's the other way round. One person shows gratitude, and the rest go on their way without a second thought.

And this time it's a Samaritan...

As before, we come close in the crowd and pick up the vibes. Here we are, in quite tricky territory. (Actually, it's still tricky today to pick your way around the borderlands in what used to be called the West Bank.) Nobody quite knows who's going to be friendly and who's likely to be hostile. One place they may welcome you, another they may throw stones.

The group coming towards us now aren't hostile. They're asking for help... but then we see who they are. And what they are. They are... lepers! Horrors! Don't let them come near me! Look at their hands, all maimed, fingers missing. Look at that man's face – half of it's eaten away! Send them away, quickly!

(That reaction, by the way, was typical in those days, which is why the men stayed at a distance from Jesus and his party. It is still, sadly, typical of many today, who don't realize that 'leprosy' is a loose word for several powerful, but often curable, skin diseases.)

Now the word on the street is that on a previous occasion Jesus actually *touched* someone like that. We're glad he didn't do that this time – though, granted, that previous occasion they say the man was cured. All he does is tell them to go and show themselves to the priests. But isn't that what you do *after* you're cured, not before, so they can give you a clean bill of health? What is he thinking of?

Anyway, off they go. We stand there, puzzled, wondering if we had a lucky escape or if, on this occasion, Jesus just wanted to be rid of them. But no, wrong as usual. One of them's coming back – and he's cured! Something's happened to him! Jesus was giving them a test of faith, and he's passed it wonderfully.

So here he comes, running up to us and falling down in front of Jesus, praising God at the top of his voice…and his accent gives him away. He's one of Them. He's a foreigner. A Samaritan. Typical. Just when we thought we had Jesus figured out – he's the Messiah for us Jews, right? – it turns out he's pushing the boundaries, opening the gates to all the other lot as well. But what's he saying? 'Your faith has saved you'? Well, but don't I have faith too? So has my faith had that effect? How would I know? Perhaps one sign might be if I started to see things the way Jesus does…

Today

Gracious Lord, teach me to see with your eyes of compassion, and teach me to love people with your healing and welcoming love.

WEEK 5: TUESDAY

Luke 18; focused on 18.9–14

[9]He told this next parable against those who trusted in their own righteous standing and despised others.

[10]'Two men', he said, 'went up to the Temple to pray. One was a Pharisee, the other was a tax-collector. [11]The Pharisee stood

and prayed in this way to himself: "God, I thank you that I am not like the other people – greedy, unjust, immoral, or even like this tax-collector. ¹²I fast twice in the week; I give tithes of all that I get."

¹³"But the tax-collector stood a long way off, and didn't even want to raise his eyes to heaven. He beat his breast and said, "God, be merciful to me, sinner that I am." ¹⁴Let me tell you, he was the one who went back to his house vindicated by God, not the other. Don't you see? People who exalt themselves will be humbled, and people who humble themselves will be exalted.'

So let's get this straight. You've worked hard all your life. You've always played the game by the rules. Never done anyone a bad turn. Never cheated on your tax returns. Never told a white lie in court to get a friend off a charge. Never, *never* even *dreamed* of going off with someone else's wife. And yes, you've always known what the law required. Studied it carefully. Listened to the best teachers. Done your best to keep yourself and your family absolutely on track. If the law says you fast on Wednesdays and Fridays, then you fast on Wednesdays and Fridays. If the law says you calculate exactly a tenth of all your income and give that to God, that's what you do.

Something of a sigh of relief, isn't it? You now know that when you go up to the Temple to say your prayers, you're in the clear. God is going to be very happy that you're there. After all, you're the sort of person who makes the world go round in the right way. You're the sort who, if only there were enough of you doing it, would speed up the arrival of God's kingdom. So now, come to the Temple and say your prayers. 'Thank you, God, that I am me.'

A bit near the bone for some of us? Perhaps. It certainly was for several of Jesus' hearers. Even if they were used to his standing the world on its head, it was surely a bit much for him to have a go at this respectable, proper, scrupulous Pharisee. Wasn't the poor chap simply doing what God had told him to?

Well, from one point of view, yes. But Jesus was constantly nudging people, or positively shoving them, towards seeing everything differently. Prayer is about loving God, and the deepest Jewish traditions insist that loving God is something you do with heart, mind, soul and strength, and your neighbour as yourself, not calculating whether you've done everything just right and feeling smug because your neighbour hasn't managed it so well.

So how are you going to pray?

'Lord, have mercy on me, a sinner.'

Some people think that's a bit morose. Can't you move on from that? Well, yes: when you hear Jesus' words saying, 'This was the man who went home in the right with God!' But that's a free gift from God, not something you've cobbled together by your own hard work. That's what the good news is all about.

Many people find that praying that prayer, or one like it, can go right down into the heart, into your breathing and feeling, into your loving and longing, waiting and hoping. It isn't morose at all. It looks with love and gratitude to Jesus himself, and constantly turns away from its own achievements to accept and celebrate God's grace.

Today

How are you going to pray today? Who are you like?

WEEK 5: WEDNESDAY

Luke 19; focused on 19.1–10

[1]They went into Jericho and passed through. [2]There was a man named Zacchaeus, a chief tax-collector, who was very rich. [3]He was trying to see who Jesus was, but, being a small man, he couldn't, because of the crowd. [4]So he ran on ahead, along the route Jesus was going to take, and climbed up into a sycamore tree to see him.

⁵When Jesus came to the place, he looked up.

'Zacchaeus,' he said to him, 'hurry up and come down. I have to stay at your house today.' ⁶So he hurried up, came down, and welcomed him with joy.

⁷Everybody began to murmur when they saw it. 'He's gone in to spend time with a proper old sinner!' they were saying.

⁸But Zacchaeus stood there and addressed the Master.

'Look, Master,' he said, 'I'm giving half my property to the poor. And if I have defrauded anyone of anything, I'm giving it back to them four times over.'

⁹'Today,' said Jesus, 'salvation has come to this house, because he too is a son of Abraham. ¹⁰You see, the son of man came to seek and to save the lost.'

Think back to how it was. It's hot in Jericho, even in the spring as Passover approaches. Crowds all around, pilgrims going to Jerusalem. Everybody excited. Nearly there now; more people joining the procession all the time.

Jesus, as usual, keeps surprising us. Sometimes he's chatty, particularly with the unlikely people we meet. He makes friends, has a way with folk. But sometimes he strides on ahead as if he can see something we can't see, something he has to set his face at, to summon up determination. Perhaps he'd rather, actually, stay here in the Jordan valley where everybody seems happy to have him around. Perhaps he knows something we don't about what's likely to happen in Jerusalem when we get there...

Anyway, in Jericho everyone knows everyone else's business, and everyone certainly knows Zacchaeus. Mind you, all tax-collectors are the same: the Romans force them to do the job, demand a fixed sum, and don't mind how they get it or how much they claw in for themselves while they're at it. Forcing us to part with our hard-earned cash *and* working for the occupying forces; no wonder Zacchaeus has extra bolts on his doors and windows. I suppose he's used to the whispers in the street...Maybe people have always laughed at him because he's small, so he doesn't mind it now when they spit on the ground after he's gone by.

But now, there he is, scrambling up that tree! Well, that's certainly got everybody's attention. Including Jesus. He'll probably just grin and walk by. But no! He's stopping and talking to him...and they're going off together! What on earth is this about? Another party, I suppose. With the wrong people, again.

Yes: the whispers are starting again, in earnest. 'He's having lunch with one of Them! With a traitor! A sinner! Someone who's letting the side down – who's letting God down!' We all join in. Jesus is supposed to be a pilgrim on the way to the holy city for an important festival. He shouldn't be getting his hands dirty with rubbish like that.

But then the door flies open again and Zacchaeus comes out with Jesus. He wants to say something for everyone to hear. 'It's all going to be different now,' he says. 'I'm giving half of everything away. And I'm going to pay back fourfold anyone I've cheated.'

Then Jesus says it. We thought he was on pilgrimage to Jerusalem, but this was his real mission. 'This is what I came for – to look for the lost and to rescue them.' Well, he's made a lot of people happy in Jericho.

But now, as we look back from a few weeks later, we realize that something else was going on as well. Zacchaeus climbed a tree to see Jesus – and he discovered the meaning of salvation. Jesus was on his way to hang on a very different tree. And that was how salvation happened.

Today

Imagine you are Zacchaeus and Jesus comes to your house. Who talks first? What would you want to say to Jesus? What would it be like, meeting him?

WEEK 5: THURSDAY
Luke 20; focused on 20.9–19

⁹Jesus began to tell the people this parable. 'There was a man who planted a vineyard, let it out to tenant farmers, and went abroad for a long while. ¹⁰When the time came, he sent a slave to the farmers to collect from them some of the produce of the vineyard. But the farmers beat him and sent him away empty-handed. ¹¹He then sent a further slave, and they beat him, abused him, and sent him back empty-handed. ¹²Then he sent yet a third, and they beat him up and threw him out.

¹³'So the master of the vineyard said, "What shall I do? I'll send my beloved son. They will certainly respect him!" ¹⁴But when the farmers saw him they said to each other, "This is the heir! Let's kill him, and then the inheritance will belong to us!" ¹⁵And they threw him out of the vineyard and killed him.

'So what will the master of the vineyard do? ¹⁶He will come and wipe out those farmers, and give the vineyard to others.'

When they heard this, they said, 'God forbid!' ¹⁷But Jesus looked round at them and said, 'What then does it mean in the Bible when it says,

'"The very stone the builders refused
Now for the corner's top is used"?

¹⁸'Everyone who falls on that stone will be smashed to smithereens; but if it falls on anyone, it will crush them.'

¹⁹The scribes and the chief priests tried to lay hands on him then and there. But they were afraid of the people, because they knew that Jesus had told this parable against them.

Here in the North-East of England one or two folk songs are woven tightly into our culture. One of them, 'The Blaydon Races', functions almost as a national anthem. It's the musical equivalent of the Angel of the North.

But supposing someone, one day, sang it and gave it some new words?

Oh, me lads, you should have seen us gannin'
Passin' the folks alang the road, just as they were stannin'
There were lots of lads and lasses there, all wi' frowning faces
Gannin' alang the London Road – to flee the Blaydon Races!

Suddenly the story stands on its head. Instead of everybody going to the races to have a good time, they are trying to escape! No doubt subsequent verses will tell us why…

Now in Jesus' culture there were several stories, and several songs, which people knew just as well as we in the North-East know 'The Blaydon Races' (with the proper words, of course). One of those stories comes in the form of an old poem about God's vineyard. (It's in Isaiah 5.) It's a lament: God has planted a vineyard, but the vineyard has gone to the bad and is producing wild grapes. So God will come and tear it down, and let the thorns and brambles take it over. And all because the people of Israel had exchanged justice for violence, and uprightness for wickedness.

Now here's the new twist. It brings the whole thing bang up to date. The vineyard owner has let it out to tenants, and sends a string of servants to get the fruit – and the tenants ill-treat them. He then sends his one and only son, and they kill him. So now the story has a different ending. Instead of the vineyard going to rack and ruin, it's the tenants, and the vineyard is transferred to new ones.

What does it mean? Jesus quotes another well-known song, this time a psalm for pilgrims on their way to Jerusalem. It sings of going up to the Temple, and about the odd-shaped stone that won't fit anywhere in the building except the top of the corner. Jesus links it with yet another well-known local story, the dream-vision in Daniel 2, which speaks of the stone that will crush all opposition and then become a mountain that will fill the whole earth.

Why is he talking in these riddles, rooted in scripture but all with a new twist?

Well, something new is happening, so massive, dangerous and unbelievable that the only way you can talk about it is through these old songs and stories. As we watch the action and try to work it out, we realize that if we're going to make sense of what comes next we too will need to think and pray our way through the scriptures. Jesus, at least, seems to think that's the way to understand what he's going to do next – and what the tenants are going to do to him, the Beloved Son.

Today

If this parable were to be told today, who would be the tenants, and what would Jesus be saying to them?

WEEK 5: FRIDAY
Luke 21; focused on 21.7–19

[7]'Teacher,' they asked him, 'when will these things happen? What will be the sign that it's all about to take place?'

[8]'Watch out that nobody deceives you,' said Jesus. 'Yes: lots of people will come using my name, saying "I'm the one!" and "The time has come!" Don't go following them. [9]When you hear about wars and rebellions, don't be alarmed. These things have to happen first, but the end won't come at once.

[10]'One nation will rise against another,' he went on, 'and one kingdom against another. [11]There will be huge earthquakes, famines and plagues in various places, terrifying omens, and great signs from heaven.

[12]'Before all this happens they will lay hands on you and persecute you. They will hand you over to the synagogues and prisons. They will drag you before kings and governors because of my name. [13]That will become an opportunity for you to tell

your story. [14]So settle it in your hearts not to work out beforehand what tale to tell; [15]I'll give you a mouth and wisdom, which none of your opponents will be able to resist or contradict.

[16]'You will be betrayed by parents, brothers and sisters, relatives and friends, and they will kill some of you. [17]You will be hated by everyone because of my name. [18]But no hair of your head will be lost. [19]The way to keep your lives is to be patient.'

If you drive towards Durham, the great cathedral city at the heart of the North-East of England, you will see road signs indicating a cathedral. The signs don't actually look like Durham Cathedral. They have a conventional symbol that means 'cathedral', even if it doesn't look like any one of them in particular.

People find it easy to decode signs like that and other symbols, too. When a cartoon in the newspaper makes one politician look like a crocodile and another like a frightened fish trying to escape, we don't need someone to explain patiently how the picture works.

But it's harder to understand symbols when we read books. Particularly when those books come from another time and place. We are like a visitor from Mars trying to make sense of human road signs or newspaper cartoons.

So what is Jesus saying here? And what is Luke telling us through it? And how do we pray our way into a passage like this, full of such dark and strange stuff?

First, Jesus is inviting his hearers (and Luke is inviting his readers) to face the future with confidence. All sorts of frightening things are going to happen, but that doesn't mean God isn't in control, or that we are going to be knocked off our feet. Our part is to have faith, patience and courage.

Second, Jesus is telling the disciples, in symbolic language taken from the Old Testament, that political and military up-heavals are going to take place, at the climax of which Jerusalem itself will be destroyed. (Read the whole chapter, and you'll see that this is what it's about.) Jerusalem had been, for a thousand years, the place where God's people had gone to worship him. But the city itself had become an idol, and the evidence for that was its refusal to accept Jesus and his way of peace (see 19.41– 44). Jesus himself would now be the place where, and the means by which, God meets with his people.

Third, as all this is happening, God's people will suffer. They will be caught between the old age and the new one. That's a deeply uncomfortable place to be.

Fourth, the church from quite early on read this passage, and others like it, not as referring to the fall of Jerusalem, but to the end of the present age. That wasn't what Jesus originally had in mind, but it makes good sense anyway. We, too, are called to live between the old age and the new, and to pray in faith, courage and patience for God's purposes to come to pass.

Even if we can only describe them in picture-language.

Today

Think about those whose faith may get knocked and battered by what is going on around them. Pray for them, that God will help them to hold on.

You may want to talk to God about the things that knock and batter you and your faith, too.

WEEK 5: SATURDAY
Luke 22.1—23.49

[1]The time came for the festival of unleavened bread, known as Passover. [2]The chief priests and the scribes looked for a way to assassinate Jesus, a difficult task because of the crowds.

[3]The satan entered into Judas, whose surname was Iscariot, who was one of the company of the Twelve. [4]He went and held a meeting with the chief priests and officers, to discuss how he

might hand Jesus over. [5]They were delighted, and promised to pay him. [6]He agreed, and started to look for an opportunity to hand him over to them when the crowds weren't around.

[7]The day of unleavened bread arrived, the day when people had to kill the Passover lamb. [8]Jesus dispatched Peter and John.

'Off you go,' he said, 'and get the Passover ready for us to eat.'

[9]'Where d'you want us to prepare it?' they asked him.

[10]'Listen carefully,' said Jesus. 'As you go into the city a man will meet you carrying a jar of water. Follow him, and when he goes into a house, go after him. [11]Then say to the householder there, "The teacher says, 'Where is the living-room where I can eat the Passover with my disciples?'" [12]And he will show you a large upstairs room, laid out and ready. Make the preparations there.'

[13]So they went and found it as he had said to them, and they prepared the Passover.

[14]When the time came, Jesus sat down at table, and the apostles with him.

[15]'I have been so much looking forward to eating this Passover with you before I have to suffer,' he said to them. [16]'For – let me tell you – I won't eat it again until it's fulfilled in the kingdom of God.'

[17]Then he took a cup, and gave thanks, and said, 'Take this and share it among yourselves. [18]Let me tell you, from now on I won't drink from the fruit of the vine until the kingdom of God comes.'

[19]Then he took some bread. He gave thanks, broke it and gave it to them.

'This is my body,' he said, 'which is given for you. Do this in memory of me.'

[20]So too, after supper, with the cup: 'This cup', he said, 'is the new covenant, in my blood which is shed for you.

[21]'But look here! The hand of the one who will betray me is with me at this table. [22]The son of man is indeed going, as it is marked out for him; but woe betide that man by whom he is betrayed!'

[23]They began to ask each other which of them was going to do this.

²⁴A quarrel began among them: which of them was to be seen as the most important?

²⁵'Pagan kings lord it over their subjects,' said Jesus to them, 'and people in power get themselves called "Benefactors". ²⁶That's not how it's to be with you. The most important among you ought to be like the youngest. The leader should be like the servant. ²⁷After all, who is the more important, the one who sits at table or the one who waits on him? The one at table, obviously! But I am with you here like a servant.

²⁸'You are the ones who have stuck it out with me through the trials I've had to endure. ²⁹This is my bequest to you: the kingdom my Father bequeathed to me! ³⁰What does this mean? You will eat and drink at my table, in my kingdom, and you will sit on thrones, judging the twelve tribes of Israel.

³¹'Simon, Simon, listen to this. The satan demanded to have you. He wanted to shake you into bits like wheat. ³³But I prayed for you; I prayed that you wouldn't run out of faith. And, when you turn back again, you must give strength to your brothers.'

³³'Master,' replied Simon, 'I'm ready to go with you to prison – or to death!'

³⁴'Let me tell you, Peter,' replied Jesus, 'the cock won't crow today before you have three times denied that you know me.'

³⁵'When I sent you out,' Jesus said to them, 'without purse or bag or sandals, were you short of anything?'

'Nothing,' they replied.

³⁶'But now,' he said, 'anyone who has a purse should take it, and the same with a bag. And anyone who doesn't have a sword should sell his cloak and buy one. ³⁷Let me tell you this: when the Bible says, "He was reckoned with the lawless," it must find its fulfilment in me. Yes; everything about me must reach its goal.'

³⁸'Look, Master,' they said, 'we've got a couple of swords here.'

'That's enough!' he said to them.

³⁹So off they went. Jesus headed, as usual, for the Mount of Olives, and his disciples followed him.

⁴⁰When he came to the place, he said to them, 'Pray that you won't come into the trial.'

⁴¹He then withdrew from them about a stone's throw, and knelt down to pray.

⁴²'Father,' he said, 'if you wish it – please take this cup away from me! But it must be your will, not mine.' ⁴³An angel appeared to him from heaven, strengthening him. ⁴⁴By now he was in agony, and he prayed very fervently. And his sweat became like clots of blood, falling on the ground. ⁴⁵Then he got up from praying, and came to the disciples and found them asleep because of sorrow.

⁴⁶'Why are you sleeping?' he said to them. 'Get up and pray, so that you won't come into the trial.'

⁴⁷While he was still speaking, a crowd appeared. The man named Judas, one of the Twelve, was leading them. He came towards Jesus to kiss him, ⁴⁸but Jesus said to him, 'Judas! Are you going to betray the son of man with a kiss?'

⁴⁹Jesus' followers saw what was about to happen.

'Master!' they said. 'Shall we go in with the swords?' ⁵⁰And one of them struck the high priest's servant, and cut off his right ear.

⁵¹'Enough of that!' said Jesus, and healed the ear with a touch.

⁵²Then Jesus spoke to the chief priests, the Temple guardsmen, and the elders who had come after him.

'Anyone would think I was a brigand,' he said, 'for you to come out with swords and clubs! ⁵³Every day I've been in the Temple with you and you never laid hands on me. But your moment has come at last, and so has the power of darkness.'

⁵⁴So they arrested Jesus, took him off, and brought him into the high priest's house. Peter followed at a distance. ⁵⁵They lit a fire in the middle of the courtyard and sat around it, and Peter sat in among them.

⁵⁶A servant-girl saw him sitting by the fire. She stared hard at him. 'This fellow was with him!' she said.

⁵⁷Peter denied it. 'I don't know him, woman,' he said.

⁵⁸After a little while another man saw him and said, 'You're one of them!'

'No, my friend, I'm not,' replied Peter.

⁵⁹After the space of about an hour, another man insisted, 'It's true! This man was with him; he's a Galilean too!'

⁶⁰'My good fellow,' said Peter, 'I don't know what you're talking about.' And at once, while he was still speaking, the cock crowed. ⁶¹The Master turned and looked at Peter, and Peter called to mind the words the Master had spoken to him: 'Before the cock crows, this very day, you will deny me three times.' ⁶²And he went outside and wept bitterly.

⁶³The men who were holding Jesus began to make fun of him and knock him about. ⁶⁴They blindfolded him.

'Prophesy!' they told him. 'Who is it that's hitting you?'

⁶⁵And they said many other scandalous things to him.

⁶⁶When the day broke, the official assembly of the people, the chief priests and the scribes came together, and they took him off to their council.

⁶⁷'If you are the Messiah,' they said, 'tell us!'

'If I tell you,' he said to them, 'you won't believe me. ⁶⁸And if I ask you a question, you won't answer me. ⁶⁹But from now on the son of man will be seated at the right hand of God's power.'

⁷⁰'So you're the son of God, are you?' they said.

'You say that I am,' he said to them.

⁷¹'Why do we need any more witnesses?' they said. 'We've heard it ourselves, from his own mouth!'

23 ¹The whole crowd of them got up and took Jesus to Pilate.

²They began to accuse him. 'We found this fellow', they said, 'deceiving our nation! He was forbidding people to give tribute to Caesar, and saying that he is the Messiah – a king!'

³So Pilate asked Jesus, 'You are the king of the Jews?'

'You said it,' replied Jesus.

⁴'I find no fault in this man,' said Pilate to the chief priests and the crowds. ⁵But they became insistent.

'He's stirring up the people,' they said, 'teaching them throughout the whole of Judaea. He began in Galilee, and now he's come here.'

[6]When Pilate heard that, he asked if the man was indeed a Galilean. [7]When he learned that he was from Herod's jurisdiction he sent him to Herod, who happened also to be in Jerusalem at that time.

[8]When Herod saw Jesus he was delighted. He had been wanting to see him for quite some time now, since he'd heard about him, and hoped to see him perform some sign or other. [9]He questioned him this way and that, but Jesus gave no answer at all. [10]The chief priests and the scribes stood by, accusing him vehemently. [11]Herod and his soldiers treated Jesus with contempt; they ridiculed him by dressing him up in a splendid robe, and sent him back to Pilate. [12]And so it happened, that very day, that Herod and Pilate became friends with each other. Up until then, they had been enemies.

[13]So Pilate called the chief priests, the rulers and the people. [14]'You brought this man before me,' he said to them, 'on the grounds that he was leading the people astray. Look here, then: I examined him in your presence and I found no evidence in him of the charges you're bringing against him. [15]Nor did Herod; he sent him back to me. Look: there is no sign that he's done anything to deserve death. [16]So I'm going to flog him and let him go.'

[18]'Take him away!' they shouted out all together. 'Release Barabbas for us!' [19](Barabbas had been thrown into prison because of an uprising that had taken place in the city, and for murder.) [20]Pilate spoke to them again, with the intention of letting Jesus go, [21]but they shouted back, 'Crucify him! Crucify him!'

[22]'Why?' he said for the third time. 'What's he done wrong? I can't find anything he's done that deserves death, so I'm going to beat him and let him go.'

[23]But they went on shouting out at the tops of their voices, demanding that he be crucified; and eventually their shouts won

the day. ²⁴Pilate gave his verdict that their request should be granted. ²⁵He released the man they asked for, the one who'd been thrown into prison because of rebellion and murder, and gave Jesus over to their demands.

²⁶As they led him away, they grabbed a man from Cyrene called Simon, who was coming in to the city from outside, and they forced him to carry the crossbeam behind Jesus. ²⁷A great crowd of the people followed Jesus, including women who were mourning and wailing for him. ²⁸Jesus turned and spoke to them.

'Daughters of Jerusalem,' he said, 'don't cry for me. Cry for yourselves instead! Cry for your children! ²⁹Listen: the time is coming when you will say, "A blessing on the barren! A blessing on wombs that never bore children, and breasts that never nursed them!" ³⁰At that time people will start to say to the mountains, "Fall on us," and to the hills, "Cover us"! ³¹Yes: if this is what they do with the green tree, what will happen to the dry one?'

³²Two other criminals were taken away with him to be executed. ³³When they came to the place called The Skull, they crucified him there, with the criminals, one on his right and one on his left.

³⁴'Father,' said Jesus, 'forgive them! They don't know what they're doing!'

They divided his clothes, casting lots for them.

³⁵The people stood around watching. The rulers hurled abuse at him.

'He rescued others,' they said, 'let him try rescuing himself, if he really is the Messiah, God's chosen one!'

³⁶The soldiers added their taunts, coming up and offering him cheap wine.

³⁷'If you're the king of the Jews,' they said, 'rescue yourself!'

³⁸The charge was written above him: 'This is the King of the Jews.'

³⁹One of the bad characters who was hanging there began to insult him. 'Aren't you the Messiah?' he said. 'Rescue yourself – and us, too!'

⁴⁰But the other one told him off. 'Don't you fear God?' he said. 'You're sharing the same fate that he is! ⁴¹In our case it's fair enough; we're getting exactly what we asked for. But this fellow hasn't done anything out of order.

⁴²'Jesus,' he went on, 'remember me when you finally become king.'

⁴³'I'm telling you the truth,' replied Jesus, 'you'll be with me in paradise, this very day.'

⁴⁴By the time of the sixth hour, darkness came over all the land. ⁴⁵The sunlight vanished until the ninth hour. The veil of the Temple was ripped down the middle. ⁴⁶Then Jesus shouted out at the top of his voice, 'Here's my spirit, Father! You can take care of it now!' And with that he died.

⁴⁷The centurion saw what happened, and praised God.

'This fellow', he said, 'really was in the right.'

⁴⁸All the crowds who had come together for the spectacle saw what happened, and they went away beating their breasts. ⁴⁹Those who knew Jesus, including the women who had followed him from Galilee, remained at a distance and watched the scene.

The story is so powerful, so overwhelming, that we might be tempted to leave it without comment, and just say, 'Read it.' Read it on your knees; read it slowly; read it and identify yourself with one of the characters. (Peter? Pilate? The centurion? There's quite a choice.) Read it fast to get the dramatic flow; read it and ask yourself: What would I have thought if I'd been there?

The first thought that might strike you (and Luke wants it to) is that this was a massive miscarriage of justice. Jesus was innocent, condemned on charges that were obviously trumped up. Other people had been doing the things he was accused of – not least Barabbas, guilty of murder and revolt. Jesus was not guilty. As the centurion said, he was in the right all along.

The second thought that might occur to you (and again Luke intends that it should) is that there is a strange to-and-fro between what happens to Jesus and what, as he still insists, is going to happen to the city and its inhabitants. He has warned again and again, ever since chapter 13 at least, that if Jerusalem refuses to listen to his urgent message there will be dire consequences.

When Pontius Pilate sent in the troops to kill Galilean pilgrims, and when the Tower of Siloam fell on eighteen people, that was just an advance signpost to what swords and falling stonework would do when the city itself fell to the Romans. But Jesus is going ahead, as a Galilean pilgrim, taking Pilate's verdict upon himself. As he said, he was like a green tree, not ready for burning; all around him were dry sticks, young firebrands eager for revolt, ready to rush in crazy boldness against the might of Rome. But he was going ahead of them, taking the full force of Roman anger against himself, so that they wouldn't have to have it land on them. Unless they so chose.

The third thing that Luke hopes will dawn on you is that when Jesus celebrated his last meal with his followers he intended it to be a meal that would explain what was going to happen. He wanted to explain his forthcoming death, not by providing a theory for us to get our minds around but a meal for us to share. Jesus didn't die so that we could have right ideas. He died so that we could live. His death is like food and drink: Passover food and drink, God's food and drink for God's freedom-people.

That's just the beginning. As you identify with this or that character, you will see more. Above all, you will see Jesus himself, reaching the point he knew had to come. This, he believed, was how God's kingdom would be brought about, on earth as in heaven.

It wasn't what people were expecting. But Jesus believed it was what the scriptures had said all along.

Today

Let this great story fill your imagination, so that it will colour your thinking and feeling whatever you're doing and whatever happens.

HOLY WEEK: PALM SUNDAY

Psalm 31.9–16

[9]Be gracious to me, O Lord, for I am in distress;
    my eye wastes away from grief, my soul and body also.
[10]For my life is spent with sorrow, and my years with sighing;
    my strength fails because of my misery,
    and my bones waste away.
[11]I am the scorn of all my adversaries,
    a horror to my neighbours,
    an object of dread to my acquaintances;
    those who see me in the street flee from me.
[12]I have passed out of mind like one who is dead;
    I have become like a broken vessel.
[13]For I hear the whispering of many – terror all around! –
    as they scheme together against me,
    as they plot to take my life.
[14]But I trust in you, O Lord;
    I say, 'You are my God.'
[15]My times are in your hand;
    deliver me from the hand of my enemies and persecutors.
[16]Let your face shine upon your servant;
    save me in your steadfast love.

There is nowhere – no, not the darkest and loneliest place on the earth – where the Psalmists have not been before us. Here, as in some other places like Psalms 22, 69 and 88, we find the writer in the pit of despair.

Some of us have been there, too. Others may not have been, but part of the point of praying the Psalms is that we can identify, in our prayers, with people who are passing through exactly that kind of trial right now. And, in particular, we come today to share in prayer in the final struggles and horrors faced by Jesus himself as he went on his lonely journey to the cross.

The honesty of the despairing complaint is all-important. There is no point pretending that things really aren't that bad when actually they are. Layer after layer of misery appears before our eyes: the writer is physically weak through overwhelming sadness (verses 9 and 10), a social outcast and, worse, forgotten altogether (verses 11 and 12); and, as if all else were not enough, he's surrounded by whispering plots aimed at finishing him off completely.

We should not hurry on too quickly to the next three verses. Instead let us pause and, in our prayer today alongside the prayer of Jesus as he goes to the cross, hold before our loving God all those around the world who are in one or more of these miseries right now. We see them on our television screens. We read about them in the newspapers. There is too much misery and we, voyeurs of other people's distress, detached and unable to help physically, can at least pray. As we stand with God's people in church today, or walk with them in a Palm Sunday procession, we can make room, in our minds, for the people who would love to be there but can't, because they are too poor, or in prison, or in a desolate country where their very lives are at risk. We should remember those who daily go about their business not knowing if a bomb, or a knife, or shell, will be the end of them.

Only when we have gathered up in our hearts a large number of sufferers from around the world (and, yes, perhaps even from among our immediate family, friends and neighbours) – only then can we proceed to the last three verses, and make them a prayer not just for ourselves and our discomforts but for God's people, for the whole human race, and indeed for the whole creation. Jesus went to the cross to draw all people to himself, and to break through the barrier of decay, despair and death, and so bring about the new purposes of the creator God for the whole of his world. We can trust this God, the God we know in this Jesus. Our times are in his hand.

Today

Pray that God's face will shine upon us, and upon his whole world, with deliverance and rescuing power.

HOLY WEEK: MONDAY

Luke 22.54–65

[54]So they arrested Jesus, took him off, and brought him into the high priest's house. Peter followed at a distance. [55]They lit a fire in the middle of the courtyard and sat around it, and Peter sat in among them.

[56]A servant-girl saw him sitting by the fire. She stared hard at him. 'This fellow was with him!' she said.

[57]Peter denied it. 'I don't know him, woman,' he said.

[58]After a little while another man saw him and said, 'You're one of them!'

'No, my friend, I'm not,' replied Peter.

[59]After the space of about an hour, another man insisted, 'It's true! This man was with him; he's a Galilean too!'

[60]'My good fellow,' said Peter, 'I don't know what you're talking about.' And at once, while he was still speaking, the cock crowed. [61]The Master turned and looked at Peter, and Peter called to mind the words the Master had spoken to him: 'Before the cock crows, this very day, you will deny me three times.' [62]And he went outside and wept bitterly.

[63]The men who were holding Jesus began to make fun of him and knock him about. [64]They blindfolded him.

'Prophesy!' they told him. 'Who is it that's hitting you?'

[65]And they said many other scandalous things to him.

I suspect most of us don't have much difficulty identifying with Peter in this story.

We all know, only too well, what it is to promise that we'll follow Jesus faithfully, that we won't let him down, that we are ready to stand firm, to suffer if necessary, and to speak up for him and his kingdom whenever required.

And then, the first time someone looks round at us with that gentle sneer – 'Oh, that's the sort of person you are! I see' – and a sardonic smile, then we back off. 'Oh no, I'm not really like that. What d'you take me for, some kind of fanatic?'

Sometimes the gentle approach – the servant-girl, hardly a threat in herself – is more telling than the full-on attack. If one of the soldiers had come up to Peter, chest to chest, Peter's natural macho brashness might have made him stand up to him. But that wouldn't have been genuine following-Jesus type of courage.

Then, once you've started down that road, it's harder to get back than you would have thought. Can't really say 'yes' to the second question if you've said 'no' to the first, can you? You will look silly and weak as well as giving the game away. And then the third time. Peter, it would have been better if you'd never come, wouldn't it?

But sometimes Jesus allows us to discover our own real weakness, even if – or perhaps especially if – it makes us ashamed.

How do you pray at that point, finding yourself inside Peter's skin when Jesus turns and looks straight at you?

Jesus himself told us, a few chapters back: 'Lord, have mercy on me, a sinner.'

You'll find that those words are as hard to say as 'No, I'm not' was easy to say a few moments earlier. But you've got to say them anyway. It's a hard step back but a short one.

But there's something else going on here as well. Something we need to grasp for when we find ourselves at the edge of the crowd when people are being rude about God, or 'religion', or Jesus, or whatever. People say all kinds of ridiculous things, and often they seem to carry the day.

As they did on this occasion. Jesus was accused, at various stages in his ministry, of being a 'false prophet', leading Israel astray. Clearly the soldiers had got wind of this. Very well, let's make him look stupid. Blindfold him, beat him about the head, and if he's a prophet he'll be able to tell us who hit him! Very clever. Very funny. They weren't the last soldiers, of course, to amuse themselves by abusing their prisoners. It's almost as though the shame that Peter was feeling at that moment was coming out into the open by being heaped onto Jesus' head.

But we know, watching the scene, that Jesus is in fact a true prophet – and that he's just proved it. 'Peter, you're going to deny me three times before cock-crow.' And he has.

Today

Paul tells us that the Lord said to him, 'My power is made perfect in weakness.' As you think about Peter in this episode, think about your own weaknesses. Offer them to God for his healing, his blessing and his strengthening.

Lord Jesus, taking my shame, knowing everything about me and still loving me, help me to learn my weaknesses and also to learn your saving and strengthening power.

HOLY WEEK: TUESDAY

Luke 22.66—23.1

[66]When the day broke, the official assembly of the people, the chief priests and the scribes came together, and they took him off to their council.

[67]'If you are the Messiah,' they said, 'tell us!'

> 'If I tell you,' he said to them, 'you won't believe me. [68]And if I ask you a question, you won't answer me. [69]But from now on the son of man will be seated at the right hand of God's power.'
>
> [70]'So you're the son of God, are you?' they said.
>
> 'You say that I am,' he said to them.
>
> [71]'Why do we need any more witnesses?' they said. 'We've heard it ourselves, from his own mouth!'
>
> 23 [1]The whole crowd of them got up and took Jesus to Pilate.

Hide in the corner as the assembly meets and, if you dare, watch and listen to the most extraordinary exchange.

They are meeting, let's remind ourselves, because over the course of the previous few days – and, before that, over the previous year or two – Jesus had been doing and saying things that were, frankly, outrageous in terms of the world-views and hopes of those in power in Jerusalem.

All of that had come to a head when he had come into the city on a donkey and had challenged their power-base by going to the Temple and throwing out the traders. The best explanation for that is that, like Jeremiah or one of the other old prophets, Jesus was acting out a powerful symbol, which he had then explained to his followers. The Temple was under God's judgment. All its meaning and history, particularly its significance as the place where God met with his people, was now being drawn to a different place. To a person.

But there's only one person, other than the high priest, who has rights over the Temple. As you hide in the corner and watch the scene, you realize how the connection has been made. It is the king who builds the Temple (think of Solomon), or who has the right to declare its future. And the king means the Messiah, the anointed one. And the Messiah, according to the scriptures, will be 'son of God'. That's what Psalm 2 had said.

All that, to them, meant rebellion of the highest order.

These connections would be obvious to them, though we have to think through them to catch their full force. But it all adds up to an explosive cocktail of accusations.

And Jesus does nothing to deflect them. Indeed, he makes matters worse. He alludes to the famous Old Testament passage (in Daniel 7) where 'one like a son of man' is brought to sit at the right hand of God himself. In other words, is given authority, under God, over the whole world.

This is the coming of the kingdom of God.

As Jesus said, he wouldn't be drinking with his friends again until God's kingdom came. This is how he believed it had to happen.

In the scene in Daniel, four mythological monsters come up out of the sea to attack God's people. The last one is the most arrogant. Then God acts, snatching up the 'one like a son of man' and vindicating him, setting him in authority.

Jesus had hinted darkly, several times before and in various ways, that all this would come true in his own life story. Now the hour had come.

Today

There are many people in the world today who face unfair courts with state prosecutors whose sole concern is to catch them out and discredit them. Pray for them, and for God's justice to flourish throughout the world.

Lord Jesus, You experienced in person torture and death as a prisoner of conscience. You were beaten and flogged and sentenced to an agonizing death though you had done no wrong. Be now with prisoners of conscience throughout the world. Be with them in their fear and loneliness, in the agony of physical and mental torture and in the face of execution and death. Stretch out your hands in power to break their chains. Be merciful to the oppressor and torturer and place a new heart within them. Forgive all injustices in our lives and transform us to be instruments of your peace, for by your wounds we are healed.

(Amnesty International)

HOLY WEEK: WEDNESDAY

Luke 23.2–25

[2]They began to accuse him. 'We found this fellow', they said, 'deceiving our nation! He was forbidding people to give tribute to Caesar, and saying that he is the Messiah – a king!'

[3]So Pilate asked Jesus, 'You are the king of the Jews?'

'You said it,' replied Jesus.

[4]'I find no fault in this man,' said Pilate to the chief priests and the crowds. [5]But they became insistent.

'He's stirring up the people,' they said, 'teaching them throughout the whole of Judaea. He began in Galilee, and now he's come here.'

[6]When Pilate heard that, he asked if the man was indeed a Galilean. [7]When he learned that he was from Herod's jurisdiction he sent him to Herod, who happened also to be in Jerusalem at that time.

[8]When Herod saw Jesus he was delighted. He had been wanting to see him for quite some time now, since he'd heard about him, and hoped to see him perform some sign or other. [9]He questioned him this way and that, but Jesus gave no answer at all. [10]The chief priests and the scribes stood by, accusing him vehemently. [11]Herod and his soldiers treated Jesus with contempt; they ridiculed him by dressing him up in a splendid robe, and sent him back to Pilate. [12]And so it happened, that very day, that Herod and Pilate became friends with each other. Up until then, they had been enemies.

[13]So Pilate called the chief priests, the rulers and the people.

[14]'You brought this man before me,' he said to them, 'on the grounds that he was leading the people astray. Look here, then: I examined him in your presence and I found no evidence in him of the charges you're bringing against him. [15]Nor did Herod;

he sent him back to me. Look: there is no sign that he's done anything to deserve death. ¹⁶So I'm going to flog him and let him go.'

¹⁸'Take him away!' they shouted out all together. 'Release Barabbas for us!' ¹⁹(Barabbas had been thrown into prison because of an uprising that had taken place in the city, and for murder.) ²⁰Pilate spoke to them again, with the intention of letting Jesus go, ²¹but they shouted back, 'Crucify him! Crucify him!'

²²'Why?' he said for the third time. 'What's he done wrong? I can't find anything he's done that deserves death, so I'm going to beat him and let him go.'

²³But they went on shouting out at the tops of their voices, demanding that he be crucified; and eventually their shouts won the day. ²⁴Pilate gave his verdict that their request should be granted. ²⁵He released the man they asked for, the one who'd been thrown into prison because of rebellion and murder, and gave Jesus over to their demands.

We last met Herod a long time ago. Or rather, we didn't meet him; we simply heard (13.31) that he was out for Jesus' blood.

Herod was 'the king of the Jews'. Not a very impressive one, granted, but he'd inherited that title from his father, 'Herod the Great', famous for lots of building projects and for killing little babies in case one of them might be the Messiah. Now the son, Herod Antipas, has been hearing rumours about Jesus for quite some time, including news that he is a prophet who can do miracles. So here's his chance! The rock musical 'Jesus Christ Superstar' gives Herod some memorable lines, inviting Jesus to do a few tricks – walk across his swimming pool, change some water into wine – that will demonstrate his power. That catches the mood exactly. Jesus is, for Herod, a kind of freak show, a would-be Messiah, but really just an oddball. And a bit of a nuisance.

So when Jesus won't co-operate with his fantasies, he does what you'd do to a mad 'messiah'. Dress him up as a king, have a good laugh, then send him off to the fate he obviously deserves.

That day, Luke remarks, Herod and Pilate became friends. The 'king of the Jews' has become the friend of the Roman empire. This is a good move politically but a bad move theologically. God's kingdom is about to be established, and it will stand over against Caesar and all his allies.

Pilate, meanwhile, is out of his depth and completely confused. He doesn't understand the finer points of Jewish expectations and hopes. All he knows is that this man is accused of being a troublemaker, but gives no sign that he is anything but sad and deluded. As we watch Jesus being brought in to the Roman governor, lonely and unprotected, after a sleepless night and rough treatment at the hands of his guards, we are bound to understand Pilate's question as deeply sarcastic.

'So! "king of the Jews", are we?'

And he's thinking: 'Anything less kingly it would be hard to imagine.'

'You've said it,' replies Jesus. 'Yes,' (in other words) 'I know you don't believe it for a moment, and I can't blame you really, because the only sort of kings you know don't look like this and don't behave like me. But it's true none the less.'

Pilate is convinced Jesus is a harmless lunatic. But the crowds think otherwise. 'Remember what he did in the Temple! He's a troublemaker. We want him dealt with.'

Finally Pilate caves in. But Luke, inviting us to share the story, wants us to know that through all these misunderstandings and blunderings God's purpose was going forward.

This was, indeed, how God's kingdom was to come.

Today

We may sometimes forget how difficult life can be for those who hold great power and authority. Sometimes they are forced to decide between what's 'right' and what will be 'popular'. Picture in your mind those you know, in our nation and elsewhere, who have that kind of responsibility. Try to look on them as Jesus looks on them; and pray for them in all that they do.

HOLY WEEK: MAUNDY THURSDAY

Luke 22.14–38

[14]When the time came, Jesus sat down at table, and the apostles with him.

[15]'I have been so much looking forward to eating this Passover with you before I have to suffer,' he said to them. [16]'For – let me tell you – I won't eat it again until it's fulfilled in the kingdom of God.'

[17]Then he took a cup, and gave thanks, and said, 'Take this and share it among yourselves. [18]Let me tell you, from now on I won't drink from the fruit of the vine until the kingdom of God comes.'

[19]Then he took some bread. He gave thanks, broke it and gave it to them.

'This is my body,' he said, 'which is given for you. Do this in memory of me.'

[20]So too, after supper, with the cup: 'This cup', he said, 'is the new covenant, in my blood which is shed for you.

[21]'But look here! The hand of the one who will betray me is with me at this table. [22]The son of man is indeed going, as it is marked out for him; but woe betide that man by whom he is betrayed!'

[23]They began to ask each other which of them was going to do this.

[24]A quarrel began among them: which of them was to be seen as the most important?

[25]'Pagan kings lord it over their subjects,' said Jesus to them, 'and people in power get themselves called "Benefactors". [26]That's not how it's to be with you. The most important among you ought to be like the youngest. The leader should be like the

servant. [27]After all, who is the more important, the one who sits at table or the one who waits on him? The one at table, obviously! But I am with you here like a servant.

[28]'You are the ones who have stuck it out with me through the trials I've had to endure. [29]This is my bequest to you: the kingdom my Father bequeathed to me! [30]What does this mean? You will eat and drink at my table, in my kingdom, and you will sit on thrones, judging the twelve tribes of Israel.

[31]'Simon, Simon, listen to this. The satan demanded to have you. He wanted to shake you into bits like wheat. [33]But I prayed for you; I prayed that you wouldn't run out of faith. And, when you turn back again, you must give strength to your brothers.'

[33]'Master,' replied Simon, 'I'm ready to go with you to prison – or to death!'

[34]'Let me tell you, Peter,' replied Jesus, 'the cock won't crow today before you have three times denied that you know me.'

[35]'When I sent you out,' Jesus said to them, 'without purse or bag or sandals, were you short of anything?'

'Nothing,' they replied.

[36]'But now,' he said, 'anyone who has a purse should take it, and the same with a bag. And anyone who doesn't have a sword should sell his cloak and buy one. [37]Let me tell you this: when the Bible says, "He was reckoned with the lawless," it must find its fulfilment in me. Yes; everything about me must reach its goal.'

[38]'Look, Master,' they said, 'we've got a couple of swords here.'

'That's enough!' he said to them.

Today we go back to the night when Jesus was betrayed, to the moment when he shared his last meal with his disciples ... Many of us will be joining with other Christians today in a solemn commemoration of this moment. 'Maundy Thursday' – the name comes from the Latin *mandatum*, the 'commandment', which, in John's gospel, Jesus gave his followers that night: the commandment that they should love one another as he had loved them.

That commandment isn't mentioned in Luke's account here, but as we ponder and pray through this story we can't help being struck by the care and love Jesus had for his friends as they blunder and bluster around, making grand promises they can't keep while failing to understand the great promises Jesus is making. Just like us, really.

Which is just as well, because otherwise we might put them on a pedestal and think, 'We could never be like that.' Sadly, we can be exactly like that: muddled, well-meaning but misguided, ready to follow Jesus one minute and deny him the next, eager to help but going about it in exactly the wrong way. So how can we pray our way into this story and make it not only our own but a means of life and hope as we keep this holy day?

First, notice the balance between the different parts of the story. It isn't just a meal, central and vital though that is. It's also a time for teaching, and modelling, Jesus' view of God's kingdom. And it's also a time for getting ready for the trials and challenges that are about to come.

Second, remind yourself, now and whenever you come to receive Communion, that this is the sign of God's *covenant* and the means of his *kingdom*. Those are big, important words and we need to roll them around in our minds. God has committed himself to his people and his world through Jesus, like a bridegroom committing himself for ever to his bride. That's what 'covenant' means, and the Communion service is like a wedding reception, celebrating the fact. And God has established, through Jesus, his saving rule over all the world. That's what 'kingdom' means – and if you think 'it doesn't look as though God's rule is actually working', read verses 25–27 again and think about the *way* God rules. He doesn't do it by sending in the tanks. He does it by calling servants.

Third, read slowly through this passage once more and note every time when, as you sit at that table with Jesus and his friends, you can sense a look of love in his eyes, now for this

106

person, now for that, now for all of them, now for you too. Love is shining out of him all the time, in his every action, even in his frustration and exasperation with them. He was Love turned into flesh. That's why we are called to love him in return, and to love one another for his sake.

Today

You may be going to Communion tonight, or sometime soon. If so, before you go, try to ponder the question, 'How will my going to Communion make me a better servant to those around me and to God's world?' And then ask yourself, 'How will my Communion equip me to face the temptations and hostility I will run into the minute I leave church?'

I once heard a wise old bishop describe Communion as a 'warrior's banquet'. It's the food we need to strengthen us to go and do the work of God's kingdom.

HOLY WEEK: GOOD FRIDAY

Luke 23.26–46

[26]As they led him away, they grabbed a man from Cyrene called Simon, who was coming in to the city from outside, and they forced him to carry the crossbeam behind Jesus.

[27]A great crowd of the people followed Jesus, including women who were mourning and wailing for him. [28]Jesus turned and spoke to them.

'Daughters of Jerusalem,' he said, 'don't cry for me. Cry for yourselves instead! Cry for your children! [29]Listen: the time is coming when you will say, "A blessing on the barren! A blessing on wombs that never bore children, and breasts that never nursed them!" [30]At that time people will start to say to the mountains, "Fall on us," and to the hills, "Cover us"! [31]Yes: if this is what they do with the green tree, what will happen to the dry one?'

[32]Two other criminals were taken away with him to be executed. [33]When they came to the place called The Skull, they

crucified him there, with the criminals, one on his right and one on his left.

[34]'Father,' said Jesus, 'forgive them! They don't know what they're doing!'

They divided his clothes, casting lots for them.

[35]The people stood around watching. The rulers hurled abuse at him.

'He rescued others,' they said, 'let him try rescuing himself, if he really is the Messiah, God's chosen one!'

[36]The soldiers added their taunts, coming up and offering him cheap wine.

[37]'If you're the king of the Jews,' they said, 'rescue yourself!'

[38]The charge was written above him: 'This is the King of the Jews.'

[39]One of the bad characters who was hanging there began to insult him. 'Aren't you the Messiah?' he said. 'Rescue yourself – and us, too!'

[40]But the other one told him off. 'Don't you fear God?' he said. 'You're sharing the same fate that he is! [41]In our case it's fair enough; we're getting exactly what we asked for. But this fellow hasn't done anything out of order.

[42]'Jesus,' he went on, 'remember me when you finally become king.'

[43]'I'm telling you the truth,' replied Jesus, 'you'll be with me in paradise, this very day.'

[44]By the time of the sixth hour, darkness came over all the land. [45]The sunlight vanished until the ninth hour. The veil of the Temple was ripped down the middle. [46]Then Jesus shouted out at the top of his voice, 'Here's my spirit, Father! You can take care of it now!' And with that he died.

One of the most moving moments at the Lambeth Conference in 2008 came when Sir Jonathan Sacks, the Chief Rabbi, gave a splendid and stirring lecture. Many of us, who had only heard him on the radio before, hadn't realized that he can not only do a brilliant three-minute 'thought for the day' but also a magisterial and moving full-scale address – part lecture, part sermon, part testimony.

In the question time that followed, one question in particular made everyone pause and hush. 'Tell us about Jesus.' What would he, a leading Jew, say about the one we call 'Messiah'?

Sir Jonathan went straight for this passage, and for verse 34, at the heart of Luke's story of the crucifixion. 'Father, forgive them; they don't know what they are doing.' At that point, he said, Jesus was echoing what the high priest says on the Day of Atonement, interceding to God for muddled and sinful Israel. Jesus, said the Chief Rabbi, was never more thoroughly Jewish than at that moment, praying for those around, praying for forgiveness, pleading the ignorance of the people as the particular reason.

As we stand back from the story, we remind ourselves that this last phase of the whole gospel had begun with Jesus coming to Jerusalem and solemnly declaring God's judgment on the Temple and its whole system. That had led to his trial before the high priest of the day, and then to Pilate and to condemnation. Jesus really does seem to have believed that it was part of his role to take into himself the task of Temple and Priest together. He would be the place where, and the means by which, God would meet with his people in grace and forgiveness.

But if Jesus on the cross is the true Priest, Luke insists that he is also the true king. This, he says, is what it looks like when God's kingdom comes! 'This is the king of the Jews'! Of course, it doesn't look like that. It looks as though he's a failed Messiah. The sneering challenge, '*If* you're the king of the Jews', goes back to the demonic challenge in the desert: '*If* you're the son of God ...'

And the point is that this moment, this bloody and dark moment, this miscarriage of justice, this terrible suffering, this offering by Jesus of his full self to the will of God – this is how

God is dealing, in sovereign, rescuing love, with the weight of the world's evil and pain, and with death itself. Jesus is the green tree, the wood that wasn't ready for burning, dying in the place of the dry trees, the people all around who were eager to bring in the kingdom in their own way rather than God's way.

So we draw all our prayers together in daring to echo that strange request made by one of the brigands alongside him: 'Jesus – remember me when you finally become king.' That's often as much as we dare say.

But Jesus surprises us, as he surprised the brigand, by his response. He *is* becoming king, here and now. No more waiting. '*Today.*' In the brigand's case: paradise now, and resurrection still to come. In our case: forgiveness, healing and hope, here and now. And the call to serve, and to give ourselves, as he gave himself for us.

Today

People still tell the story of a great mission held in the University of Oxford in 1931. Those who were there remembered one haunting, unforgettable moment, when a thousand undergraduates were *whispering*, 'Love so amazing, so divine, demands my soul, my life, my all.'

As you go about doing whatever you are doing today, you may, over and over again, like to whisper that to yourself.

'Love so amazing, so divine, demands my soul, my life, my all.'

HOLY WEEK: HOLY SATURDAY
Luke 23.50–56

[50]Now there was a man named Joseph, a member of the council. He was a good and righteous man, [51]and had not given his consent to the court's verdict or actions. He was from Arimathaea, a town in Judaea, and he was longing for God's kingdom. [52]He

approached Pilate and asked for Jesus' body. [53]He took it down, wrapped it in a shroud, and put it in a tomb hollowed out of the rock, where no one had ever been laid. [54]It was the day of Preparation, and the sabbath was beginning.

[55]The women who had followed Jesus, the ones who had come with him from Galilee, saw the tomb and how the body was laid. [56]Then they went back to prepare spices and ointments. On the sabbath they rested, as the commandment specified.

Where would you have been, that day?

Hiding in a back room somewhere, afraid to go out in case the authorities got you as well? Quite likely.

Running off into the desert, away from the city, to weep and wail and cry your eyes out because everything you had hoped for had come crashing to the ground? That sounds reasonable to me.

Sitting at home staring at the wall in a state of shock, unable to move or speak or think. Or pray. I suspect some were like that.

Holy Saturday is the moment when darkness has descended and there is nothing to make you think, 'It will be all right.' It won't. It can't be. The worst has occurred and nothing will ever be the same. That's how it feels. If you have known, this last week or this last year, a moment like that – when someone you have loved died, or when some other great tragedy swept over you like a tidal wave – then you'll have glimpsed a bit of how Jesus' followers must have felt that day.

Nobody, but nobody, was saying to themselves, 'Well, it's all right, because in three days he'll rise again as he said.' They had been expecting him to bring in God's kingdom, and never in their wildest dreams had they thought that would involve his being crucified by the pagan authorities.

But one or two people, acting perhaps out of the habits of their hearts, knew that something still had to be done.

Come into Joseph's house, that Friday evening.

'It's nearly sabbath,' says his wife.

'Yes,' he says, 'but someone has to do it.'

'Do what?' she says. 'Are you crazy? You'll get yourself killed. Anyway the body will be eaten by dogs before you know it.'

'Exactly,' he says. 'That's why someone needs to bury it. Now.'

'But where?' she says.

'In our tomb, of course,' he replies.

'Our tomb?' she says. 'But – that's meant for you and me!'

'Not now, it isn't,' he replies. 'And anyway, I'd rather we shared it with him.'

And off he goes. Pilate has had quite a bit to drink since that strange morning encounter with that very strange would-be king of the Jews, and is only too ready to grant the request.

Two or three others know what they have to do as well. Or rather, they know the first bit of what they have to do. They little think that, in being faithful in this apparently small thing, they are being prepared to be faithful in a much, much larger thing, a much greater and more thrilling task than any human has ever been given before.

Our part is to be prayerfully faithful in the small things that we can see need doing. We cannot tell what God will then do.

Today

It is a day of absolute nothingness. In catholic churches the tabernacle is left open and empty. Many churches will be completely bare. In practice, many of our churches are a hive of activity with flower arrangers and cleaners working hard to get everything ready for Easter Day.

Try to find some time today, though, to be absolutely still; to imagine Mary and the disciples utterly drained and utterly numb. Try to imagine what it must have meant to have to say, over and over again, 'Jesus is dead.'

EASTER DAY
Luke 24.1–12

¹The women went to the tomb in the very early morning of the first day of the week, carrying the spices they had prepared. ²They found the stone rolled away from the tomb, ³and when they went in they didn't find the body of the Lord Jesus.

⁴As they were at a loss what to make of it all, suddenly two men in shining clothes stood beside them. ⁵The women were terrified, and bowed their faces towards the ground.

But the men said to them, 'Why look for the living with the dead? ⁶He isn't here – he's been raised! Don't you remember? While you were still in Galilee he told you that ⁷the son of man must be handed over into the hands of sinners, and be crucified, and rise again on the third day.'

⁸And they remembered his words.

⁹They went back, away from the tomb, and told all this to the eleven and all the others. ¹⁰It was Mary Magdalene, Joanna, and Mary the wife of James, and the others with them. They said this to the apostles; ¹¹and this message seemed to them just stupid, useless talk, and they didn't believe them.

¹²Peter, though, got up and ran to the tomb. He stooped down and saw only the grave-clothes. He went back home, perplexed at what had happened.

How does the word 'Easter' make you feel? Excited? Glad? Joyful? Relieved?

According to this story, the first answer was in fact: puzzled, terrified, unbelieving and perplexed.

I think that's good news, actually. So many people in and around church life know that they're supposed to feel happy and joyful at Eastertide but find in their hearts a little niggle – or perhaps more than a little niggle – saying, 'Are you really sure? Isn't that all very odd? And how on earth will that help pay the mortgage, save the marriage, feed the hungry, save the whales, or even make you a better Christian?'

Well, if you've got one of those little niggles today, you're in good company. Three terrified women, a bunch of frightened and grumpy disciples, and a perplexed Peter.

It all makes the point: what happened on the first Easter was something nobody expected. The challenge to pray through the Easter story is the challenge of holding your mind, and your whole life, open to the God who does unexpected things. Life-transforming things, things you'd never have imagined in your wildest dreams. Paul talks of God being able to do 'exceedingly abundantly above all that we can ask or think' (Ephesians 3.20). The power by which God can do that is precisely the power that raised Jesus from the dead (Ephesians 1.19–20).

So this story isn't yet primarily about Jesus. It's about people like us – muddled and afraid but showing up, going to look, still not understanding, but unable to let go. It's about people like us finding a stone rolled away when we thought it was impossible, but not yet understanding why it's happened or what's going to happen next. Praying at Easter isn't about celebrating with a kind of easy certainty. It's about praying in front of a world of strange new possibilities and being open to God's future.

And yet, of course, it is about Jesus as well. Before you can understand the resurrection, you have to understand what he had been trying to tell you all along, that it was *necessary* for him to go and do what he did, to take the sin, shame and death of the world onto himself. Easter, you see, isn't just an arbitrary miracle, or a moment when God says, 'Look at what amazing things I can do!' Easter is much more specific than that. It's about the new creation beginning at last, once death has done the worst that it can do.

No wonder we are easily puzzled by Easter. No wonder they were too. It doesn't fit into our easy little world-views. It explodes them all and creates a new one, God's new one, instead.

Today

In many churches, today is the day we breathe a great sigh of relief. We have got to Easter, and now we can put our feet up and relax. The clergy may even go on holiday...

But, if you think about it, Easter is where it all begins. Easter is the start, not the finish, of the new story.

As the former General Secretary of the United Nations Dag Hammarskjöld once prayed: 'For all that has been, THANKS. For all that shall be, YES!'

Gracious Lord, as we come with the women to the tomb, give us faith to stay with the story, to hold open our minds, hearts and lives to whatever you now want to do.

EASTER MONDAY

Luke 24.13–35

[13]That very day, two of them were going to a village called Emmaus, which lay about seven miles from Jerusalem. [14]They were discussing with each other all the various things that had taken place. [15]As they were discussing, and arguing with each other, Jesus himself approached and walked with them. [16]Their eyes, though, were prevented from recognizing him.

[17]'You're obviously having a very important discussion on your walk,' he said; 'what's it all about?'

They stood still, a picture of gloom. [18]Then one of them, Cleopas by name, answered him.

'You must be the only person around Jerusalem', he said, 'who doesn't know what's been going on there these last few days.'

[19]'What things?' he asked.

'To do with Jesus of Nazareth,' they said to him. 'He was a prophet. He acted with power and he spoke with power, before God and all the people. [20]Our chief priests and rulers handed him over to be condemned to death, and they crucified him. [21]But we were hoping that he was going to redeem Israel!

'And now, what with all this, it's the third day since it happened. ²²But some women from our group have astonished us. They went to his tomb very early this morning, ²³and didn't find his body. They came back saying they'd seen a vision of angels, who said he was alive. ²⁴Some of the folk with us went off to the tomb and found it just as the women had said, but they didn't see *him*.'

²⁵'You are so senseless!' he said to them. 'So slow in your hearts to believe all the things the prophets said to you! Don't you see? ²⁶This is what *had* to happen: the Messiah had to suffer, and then come into his glory!'

²⁷So he began with Moses, and with all the prophets, and explained to them the things about himself throughout the whole Bible.

²⁸They drew near to the village where they were heading. Jesus gave the impression that he was going further, ²⁹but they urged him strongly not to.

'Stay with us,' they said. 'It's nearly evening; the day is almost gone.' And he went in to stay with them.

³⁰As he was sitting at table with them he took the bread and gave thanks. He broke it and gave it to them. ³¹Then the eyes of both of them were opened, and they recognized him; and he vanished from their sight.

³²Then they said to each other, 'Do you remember how our hearts were burning inside us, as he talked to us on the road, as he opened up the Bible for us?'

³³And they got up then and there and went back to Jerusalem. There they found the eleven, and the people with them, gathered together.

³⁴They were saying, 'The Lord really has been raised! He's appeared to Simon!' ³⁵Then they told what had happened on the road, and how he was known to them in the breaking of the bread.

Perhaps Luke only tells us the name of one of the two on the road in order that the other one, left nameless, could be yours. Let's read the story like that, anyway.

So you're walking home late that day and still it doesn't make sense. We *knew* Jesus was the one! Nobody ever did or said things like he did. That makes it all the more appalling, what's happened. We had pinned all our hopes on him. This, surely, was the man God would use to rescue Israel! We talk on and on about what we saw Jesus do, about his teaching, about God's coming kingdom that we'd already begun to glimpse in him. It just doesn't make sense. Has God been playing a cruel trick on us, or what? (Whatever is making life like that for you right now, pray through this story as though it's your particular problem that you're talking about.)

And now there's someone else on the road; a stranger's come to join us. He quickly sees we're not exactly looking bright and breezy, so we explain it all again, this time to him. Our hopes. Our beliefs. Our crushing disappointment. Our sense of utter despair...'And then,' we tell him, 'just to make matters worse, some of the women came rushing in to say the tomb was empty. What's it all about? Has someone stolen his body?'

'But,' says the stranger, 'haven't you read your Bibles?'

(That's a bit much, frankly. We know the scriptures; have done since we were children. What's this about?)

'Well,' continues the stranger, 'hasn't it occurred to you that all through the Bible God allows his people to get into a real mess – slavery, defeat, despair, and finally exile in Babylon – in order to do a new thing? Isn't that what the prophets and the Psalms were about as well? Passage after passage in which Israel is promised that God will rescue them from slavery, even from sin, and sometimes even from death – but first they have to go through it and out the other side? Well then, supposing that's what had to happen to the Messiah himself, Israel's personal representative?'

You just begin to see, looming up through the mist of your sorrow and puzzlement, a new picture, a new pattern, a new possibility. It makes you feel warm deep down inside, like a hot

117

drink on a snowy day. Then – we're home! But what's our new friend going to do? We'd better invite him in.

He comes in quietly and you prepare a simple meal. Good to have a guest, especially one who can explain the Bible like that. Supposing...

But then he stops being a guest and starts acting as if he's the host. Picks up the bread and suddenly everything goes into slow motion, like it does if you fall off your donkey on the road. Where have I seen someone do that before...those eyes, that gentle, firm smile, that motion with the hands...he's breaking the bread...and then, all in a rush –

It's YOU! It's HIM! How come we didn't recognize...?

And then he's gone. Vanished. Didn't get up and leave. Just seemed to disappear. It's as though he could come and go between heaven and earth at will. We can still hardly believe what's happened, but we know what to do. Get back to Jerusalem! But now, instead of being gloomy, we hurry along excitedly, with that warm feeling in our hearts as we remember how he explained the Bible to us.

When we get back, we find they've heard it too! Simon Peter's seen him as well. So it isn't just us going off our heads. It's real. He's real. He's alive! So he really *was* the Messiah. And he really *has* rescued Israel. Not sure how yet, or what it's all going to mean. But this is new. The world is new. *We* are new.

Today

We can be new as well. Bring the sad stories to him. Allow him to warm your hearts with scripture. Open your eyes to see him in the breaking of the bread. That's how it's always been, and that's how it can be for us too.

Abide with us, O Lord, for it is toward evening and the day is far spent; abide with us, and with Thy whole Church. Abide with us in the evening of the day, in the evening of life, in the evening of the world. Abide with us in Thy grace and mercy, in holy Word and Sacrament, in Thy comfort and Thy blessing. Abide with us in the night of distress and fear, in the night of doubt and temptation, in the night of bitter death, when these shall overtake us. Abide with us and with all Thy faithful ones, O Lord, in time and in eternity.

(A Lutheran prayer)

EASTER TUESDAY
Luke 24.36–53

[36]As they were saying this, Jesus himself stood in the midst of them, and said, 'Peace be with you.' [37]They were terrified and alarmed, and thought they were seeing a ghost.

[38]'Why are you so disturbed?' he said. 'Why do these questionings come up in your hearts? [39]Look at my hands and feet; it really is me, myself. Touch me and see! Ghosts don't have flesh and bones like you can see I have.'

[40]With these words, he showed them his hands and feet.

[41]While they were still in disbelief and amazement from sheer joy, he said to them, 'Have you got something here to eat?' [42]They gave him a piece of baked fish, [43]which he took and ate in front of them.

[44]Then he said to them, 'This is what I was talking to you about when I was still with you. Everything written about me in the law of Moses, and in the prophets and the psalms, had to be fulfilled.' [45]Then he opened their minds to understand the Bible.

[46]'This is what is written,' he said: 'the Messiah must suffer and rise from the dead on the third day, [47]and in his name repentance, for the forgiveness of sins, must be announced to all the nations, beginning from Jerusalem. [48]You are the witnesses for all this. [49]Now, look: I'm sending upon you what my Father has promised. But stay in the city until you are clothed with power from on high.'

⁵⁰Then he took them out as far as Bethany, and lifted up his hands and blessed them. ⁵¹As he was blessing them, he was separated from them and carried into heaven.

⁵²They worshipped him, and went back to Jerusalem in great joy. ⁵³They spent all their time in the Temple, praising God.

When was the last time you heard someone say 'Get real!'?

There are lots of fantasy worlds out there. If people insist on living in them they are going to be more and more out of touch with genuine reality.

Some people think that's what it's like being a Christian. But if you learn to live in the world of Luke's story you'll discover that the opposite is true. This story is about reality. *Real* reality.

This closing passage begins with the reality of the risen Jesus. The disciples knew all about ghosts, visions, hallucinations. The ancient world and its literature are full of stories about that kind of thing. It was natural for Jesus' followers, still stunned and shaken by all that had happened, to suppose that they were 'seeing things', as we put it.

Jesus offers them two signs that this isn't the case. It's like pinching yourself to see if you're dreaming.

First, he shows them his hands and his feet and invites them to touch him. They feel the marks of the nails: not only the signs that it's really him, but also the signs of his suffering, worn now as a badge of victory. He's real. He's solid. He's not a ghost. (And, at the end of the story, the fact that he disappears into heaven doesn't mean he isn't real or solid after all. It just means that 'heaven' is quite different from what many people imagine. It isn't a 'non-bodily' place. It's a different dimension of reality, too real for us normally to see or experience it.)

Second, he eats a piece of baked fish. Ghosts don't do that. Jesus' risen body is like nothing anyone has imagined before. On the one hand, it can be touched, it can eat. On the other hand, people don't instantly recognize him, and he can come and go between earth and heaven. Nobody in that world would have made all this up. They had stories about ghosts and visions and this is quite unlike any of them.

The passage then moves on to the reality of the church's mission. The resurrection doesn't mean we can now sit back and say. 'Oh, that's fine, so we haven't got anything more to do except wait for our own resurrection.' If the resurrection has launched God's new creation, God's kingdom in its new mode, then we have a job to do. A real job, a job to do with today's actual reality. 'Repentance and forgiveness' are to be announced to the nations – not just to make individuals feel sorry for their sins and seek God's pardon, but to make the nations change their ways as a whole. For that we need a bigger understanding of the reality of the Bible. That's what the risen Jesus gives his followers. We need it today as much as ever.

The final reality is worship. Heaven and earth are not far apart. In Jesus they have come together for ever. Luke wants us to respond to his entire story by finding ourselves enfolded in worship – the worship that God's people have offered to the living God, from that day to this, through the living Jesus.

That is the reality that can change all other realities in our lives, healing and transforming them once and for all.

Today

Gracious Lord, transform our lives with your risen presence and power, and teach us to praise you all our days.

EASTER WEDNESDAY

Acts 1.1–11

¹Dear Theophilus,
 The previous book that I wrote had to do with everything Jesus began to do and teach. ²I took the story as far as the day

121

when he was taken up, once he had given instructions through the Holy Spirit to his chosen apostles.

[3]He showed himself to them alive, after his suffering, by many proofs. He was seen by them for forty days, during which he spoke about God's kingdom. [4]As they were having a meal together, he told them not to go away from Jerusalem, but to wait, as he put it, 'for the Father's promise, which I was telling you about before. [5]John baptized with water, you see; but in a few days from now you will be baptized with the Holy Spirit.'

[6]So when the apostles came together, they put this question to Jesus.

'Master,' they said, 'is this the time when you are going to restore the kingdom to Israel?'

[7]'It's not your business to know about times and dates,' he replied. 'The Father has placed all that under his own direct authority. [8]What will happen, though, is that you will receive power when the Holy Spirit comes upon you. Then you will be my witnesses in Jerusalem, in all Judaea and Samaria, and to the very ends of the earth.'

[9]As Jesus said this, he was lifted up while they were watching, and a cloud took him out of their sight. [10]They were gazing into heaven as he disappeared. Then, lo and behold, two men appeared, dressed in white, standing beside them.

[11]'Galileans,' they said, 'why are you standing here staring into heaven? This Jesus, who has been taken from you into heaven, will come back in the same way you saw him go into heaven.'

What is the ascension of Jesus all about?

Some churches have a pictures of the ascension in stained-glass windows. Often they show the disciples looking up into the sky, and two feet hanging down from a cloud. It looks like a circus stunt. No wonder people find it hard to believe either that it really happened or that it means anything very much. What are we supposed to think? That Jesus went off like an astronaut into outer space, or what?

No. Heaven and earth aren't like that – and you have to understand heaven and earth if you're going to get the point of the ascension.

First, heaven and earth overlap and interlock. They go together. They are meant for each other. We have been conned by people talking as if they were a long way apart, with 'earth' being a place where space, time and matter happen and 'heaven' being a place where they don't. It's difficult, but we have to try to imagine things differently. When heaven and earth finally come together completely, the whole creation will be renewed from top to bottom (as Paul promised in Romans 8) and the entire world will be flooded with the presence and the glory of God. All that has begun to come true with Jesus.

Second, in the Bible heaven is the place from which matters on earth are run. Heaven is, as it were, the head office for supervising what goes on here on earth. People sometimes talk as if 'heaven' were far away and anybody there wouldn't care about, or be involved with, what happens here. But that's quite wrong.

Hold on, though, if heaven is where earth is managed, and if Jesus is already in heaven – why is the world still such a mess? Why isn't he sorting it all out?

The answer is staring at us out of the middle of the story.

Look again at the disciples' question (verse 6). Is this the time for God's kingdom to come, for Israel to become the leading nation of the world?

Most people think Jesus' answer is 'No.' In fact, it's a kind of 'Yes.' But, as often with Jesus, it's a 'Yes, but . . .' Yes, the kingdom is indeed coming, right now, but it's not going to look how you expected.

What will it look like, then?

Jesus' answer is designed to get us up out of our chairs and either on to our knees in prayer or into the street to get on with the job.

'You will receive power, when the Holy Spirit comes on you. Then you will be my witnesses, starting from here and reaching to the ends of the earth.'

That's not just 'telling people about Jesus so that they can come to faith', though that's how it happens person by person. We're talking about *God's kingdom* here – about God running the world in a whole new way. God wants to put the whole world the right way up. And he's promising Jesus' followers that they will have power – his own personal presence and power – so that they can be the ones through whom it happens.

That's the meaning of the ascension. Jesus goes up, the power comes down, the kingdom gets going. What are we waiting for?

Today

> There is an old Christian tradition that God sends each person into this world with a special message to deliver, with a special song to sing for others, with a special act of love to bestow. No one else can speak my message, or sing my song, or offer my act of love. These are entrusted only to me.
>
> (John Powell, *Through Seasons of the Heart*)

Take time to think about what song, message, act of love God has given *you* to bring into the world, to help God's kingdom on its way. Ask God to give you his power and his wisdom to use that gift bravely and well.

EASTER THURSDAY

Acts 2.42–47

[42]They all gave full attention to the teaching of the apostles and to the common life, to the breaking of bread and the prayers. [43]Great awe fell on everyone, and many remarkable deeds and signs were performed by the apostles.

[44]All of those who believed came together, and held everything in common. [45]They sold their possessions and belongings and

divided them up to everyone who was in need. ⁴⁶Day by day they were all together attending the Temple. They broke bread in their various houses, and ate their food with glad and sincere hearts, ⁴⁷praising God and standing in favour with all the people. And every day the Lord added to their number those who were being rescued.

Something about the way the first Christians lived was deeply attractive. They lived in a new way that made people sit up and take notice.

Luke gives us four signs of what this new way is all about.

First, the apostles' teaching. Everything about the Christian way was based on Jesus; but many newcomers who were drawn to him had never even seen him, let alone followed him around and heard his teaching. So those who had seen him needed to teach those who hadn't. All word-of-mouth stuff at this stage, but that's how that first-century culture worked anyway. No print, no electronic media: you had to use your brains and your memories. Fortunately, that's what God gave them.

Second, 'the common life', or as we sometimes say 'the fellowship'. This doesn't just mean 'nice to see you from time to time'. It means living together. True, they still physically lived in their different houses, but they behaved as one big extended family. If someone's in difficulties, there will be an aunt or uncle round the corner to turn to. If someone's in need, a relative will help out. If someone's having a celebration, you naturally invite the whole family to a party. And so on.

From quite early on, Jesus' first followers had a word for this common life: 'love'. In Greek, *agapē*. This love isn't just something that happens in your heart, in your feelings, though it certainly should be that too. It's something that happens on the street, around the table, with the children. It has to do with money, but much more than money. It's a whole shared way of life.

Third, 'the breaking of bread'. Ordinary meals, yes. But nobody who has read the story of Cleopas and his companion on the Emmaus road can think that 'breaking bread' will ever be the same again. Those whose hearts are warmed by the teaching are ready to have their eyes opened to recognize Jesus in the bread-breaking. That's how he told us to share his life together, to know him for ourselves and to be nourished by his own life.

And, fourth, 'the prayers'. The great Jewish tradition of prayer, three or more times a day, is rooted in the Psalms and other ancient scriptural praises and petitions. Only, now, Jesus is somehow part of it all. They haven't worked out yet how to begin to think of that. All they know is that, living as God's new family, the new energy bubbling up inside them is an energy that wants to praise God because of Jesus, and to pray for God's world, because Jesus is its rightful Lord.

Today

Many of us long for our churches to be different and more attractive. Sometimes we forget that we are part of our churches and that we may be part of the problem! Dream a dream today of what you long for your church to become. Ask God to help you see what *you* need to do, and (perhaps) how you need to change, to help make that dream a reality.

EASTER FRIDAY

Acts 3.1–10

¹One day, Peter and John were going up to the Temple around three o'clock in the afternoon. ²There was a man being carried in who had been lame since birth. People used to bring him every day to the Temple gate called 'Beautiful', so that he could ask for alms from folk on their way in to the Temple. ³When he saw Peter and John going in to the Temple, he asked them to give him some money. ⁴Peter, with John, looked hard at him.

'Look at us,' he said.

⁵The man stared at them, expecting to get something from them.

⁶'I haven't got any silver or gold,' Peter said, 'but I'll give you what I have got. In the name of the Messiah, Jesus of Nazareth, get up and walk!'

⁷He grabbed the man by his right hand and lifted him up. At once his feet and ankles became strong, and he leaped up, stood up and began to walk. He went in with them into the Temple, walking and jumping up and down and praising God. ⁹All the people saw him walking and praising God, ¹⁰and they knew that he was the man who had been sitting begging for alms by the Beautiful Gate of the Temple. They were filled with amazement and astonishment at what had happened to him.

The other thing that happened quite a bit in the early church was that people were healed.

We shouldn't make the obvious mistake at this point. Some people have imagined that, because God sometimes heals people in answer to prayer, it must always be God's will to heal all people in answer to prayer, so anyone who isn't then healed can't have prayed properly. Or something like that.

This must have been as much of a puzzle among the earliest Christians as it is for us. There are plenty of times in the New Testament when people get sick, or die, or other bad things happen to them, and however much they pray, and however devoutly, the answer is 'No.' Then we remember that that's what happened even to Jesus himself, in the Garden of Gethsemane. So: no easy answers. Prayer isn't an automatic machine. And sickness and trouble will be with us until God makes new heavens and new earth.

But healing happens too, and more often than sceptics like to imagine. And it happens particularly when a new work of God is going ahead, new ground is being broken, and new challenges are being faced.

We need to think a bit about what is happening in such cases. It isn't that our world and God's world are two quite different spheres, and that just occasionally God decides to 'intervene' in our world, producing something odd and irrational. It is, rather, that God, the creator, is remaking the whole world. God has dramatically and decisively achieved that in Jesus and his resurrection, and the sheer cosmic energy of that spills out, especially when his people pray, to restore and heal people in their bodies and minds as well as in their hearts and souls.

As happens so often, the man who was healed got far more than he bargained for. He was just hoping for money, but he got a whole new life. That's what it looks like when resurrection life is on the move in a community. People come to church because they want friendship, solace, companionship, a cup of tea or, yes, money. But once you ask God for help you have to be prepared for him to help you in ways you didn't expect. And also to challenge you.

Today

You, too, can be part of the work of God's new creation. What's that going to look like in your community, this Eastertide?

EASTER SATURDAY

Acts 5.27–32

[27]So they brought them and stood them in the Assembly. The high priest questioned them.

[28]'We gave you strict orders, didn't we?' he demanded. 'We told you not to teach in this Name, and look what you're doing! You have filled Jerusalem with your teaching, and you're trying to bring this man's blood on us!'

[29]'We must obey God, not humans!' responded Peter and the apostles. [30]'The God of our ancestors raised Jesus, after you had laid violent hands on him and hanged him on a tree. [31]God

exalted him to his right hand as Leader and Saviour, to give repentance to Israel and forgiveness of sins. [32]We are witnesses of these things, and so is the Holy Spirit, which God gave to those who obey him.'

What a great place to end our journey – and to begin a new one.

Come with the apostles into the Assembly. You were with them, weren't you, when that man got healed by the Beautiful Gate of the Temple? You were there when the Council told all of you not to speak or teach about Jesus any more – and when Peter told them that they had no choice, that this was just how it was to be?

It's become a power struggle now, as it was bound to be. Who's in charge around here? 'Jesus,' say the apostles. 'Us,' say the chief priests. So they can beat you and threaten you but they can't make you stop. After all, why should it be illegal to announce that Jesus is Lord, if the result is that he heals people, creates a new community, and pours out his Spirit on people so that they find their lives turned inside out?

How does that make you feel, as you stand in the Assembly and hear the officials sounding all strict and fierce? Afraid, yes. But also excited. This is real! This is what God's kingdom is all about! When God gets to work, people who have a vested interest in keeping the system running as it is are bound to get cross. (The chief priests were the wealthy aristocracy in Jerusalem.) But didn't Mary sing, all that time ago, about God putting down the mighty from their thrones, and sending the rich away empty? Didn't Jesus teach about blessings coming on the poor and woes on the rich? Could it be that it's all starting to come true? Can you think of some prayers that you might pray when you find yourself in that situation? (A hint: there's a splendid one in chapter 4.)

Now, this doesn't mean that the church can simply be 'anti-government' all the time. Things are much more cheerfully complicated than that. As you live on through the story in Acts, you'll discover that sometimes the rulers and authorities do the right thing and sometimes they don't. Sometimes, when they do, it's because the Christians have reminded them of their duty. God wants the world to be ordered, you see; otherwise the bullies will take over. But God wants them to know their place. And their place is under the rule of Jesus himself.

You now, following Jesus along with Peter and the others, discovering a new power at work but also new dangers to face, need to think clearly about these things. This is a question the church in each generation has to face. We must obey God rather than humans, and God has shown who is Leader and Saviour. There is no going back from this. But God is calling all human rulers and authorities to join in with his plans for new creation, and Christians can't simply assume that all authorities will be wicked. Many are not.

The church will find itself, again and again, caught in the middle. That's not a bad place to be. It's where Jesus himself was. Learning how to pray and act wisely, obeying God rather than human authorities, celebrating Jesus' lordship and making it come true in the real world: that's what Acts is about, that's what being resurrection people is about. That's what our Lenten journey was meant to lead to.

So this is just a start. Luke's gospel, and the book of Acts, are right at the heart of the New Testament, pointing outwards both to the other books that are there for us to enjoy and, more particularly, to the Lord Jesus himself. And to the work of his kingdom in our own day.

Today

What's going to be different now that you've lived and prayed your way through Luke's story of Jesus and the early church?

Thank God for all you've learned and pray for all those who have shared this journey with you. Pray that together we may learn how to be resurrection people, kingdom people, Jesus' people.

Printed in Great Britain
by Amazon

18078974R00084